To Dream Again

TO DREAM AGAIN

Robert D. Dale

BROADMAN PRESS
Nashville, Tennessee

4225-4l
ISBN: 0-8054-2541-1

Dewey Decimal Classification: 254
Subject headings: CHURCHES//CHURCH GROWTH

Library of Congress Catalog Card Number: 81-65386
Printed in the United States of America

Foreword

There are four ways to revitalize a church, organizationally speaking. The easiest change is policy change. You simply adjust the way you do things.

A second strategy is to change personnel. Firing the minister or electing new lay leaders is a common approach.

Another change tactic is to create new program structures. Reorganization plans are familiar in institutions of all kinds.

Change policy. Change people. Change programs. Each of these approaches has its advocates. But the approach I suggest is the most basic of all—clarify purpose.

The fourth way to revitalize a church is to define and act on its fundamental purpose. A new dream awakes a congregation. A poster motto challenges: "Aim for the sun. You may not reach it, but you will fly higher than if you never aimed at all."

This book proposes to help church leaders understand their congregations better.

The health cycle model of organization behavior I develop in this book is one way to diagnose and bring vitality to congregations. The health cycle is more intuitive than researched. I hope more empirical research will undergird this model of how it feels to live and minister within a local church or other volunteer organizations.

This book is intended for ministers and lay leaders who are

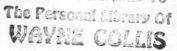

concerned for the health of their congregations—for church staff teams mapping their leader options, for interim pastors and pastor selection committees who want to match their congregation's dream with the leader skills of prospective pastors, for long-range planning committees who want to establish a base upon which to build their futuristic strategies, for missions committees who want to give a new congregation a healthy beginning, and for stagnated or stagnating churches who want to dream again. The model and principles in this book will fit most volunteer organizations and many for-profit institutions.

I owe a debt of thanks to a "cloud of witnesses" for their direct support in the growth of this book's ideas: Gayle Engels, Dave Farr, Al Persons, Eleanor Hill, Elaine Dickson, Loren Mead, Charles Woodward, Bruce Grubbs, Ken Mitchell, Dick Hester, Tony Cartledge, the faculty and students of Southeastern Baptist Theological Seminary, and minister's workshop groups around the country. Many others have encouraged from the sidelines. I'll take responsibility for the words that follow, but I thank each of you for the stimulation and feedback which gave life to this book.

All illustrations in this book are true accounts of real church situations. The names have been disguised to protect the innocent (and the guilty).

Contents

Part I
A Model of Congregational Health

1
How to Read Your Church Like a Book

Would you like to be able to read your church like a book? Here are four incidents to practice on. Can you find the common theme in these true stories?

A retired layman gives ten thousand dollars each year to Crown Hills Church. On at least two weekday mornings he is around the church, dressed in work clothes, calling himself "the church yardman," supervising the care of the lawns and shrubs. He says, "I want our church to have the most beautiful campus of any church in the nation!"

Parkwood Church has a new pastor. He disciplines himself to visit five prospective members on his way home from his church office each evening.

After a messy fight, an Old First Church splits. Even ninety-five years later, the members of Old First and Central still avoid each other. Teens from one church are forbidden to date the youth from the other congregation. When an unsuspecting area missionary accepts office space in one church's building, the other church stops contributing to area missions.

An aggressive, young minister accepts the pastorate at South Heights Church, a fast-growing suburban congregation. The rapid growth rate slows after a few months and finally becomes a trickle. The pastor alone feels frustrated. In a deacon's meeting, the pastor overhears a remark, "Well, we've finally arrived." When he inquires, he is told (for the first time) the founders of the church planned for a maximum membership of seven hundred members. That number has been reached, and the leaders are satisfied with the size of the church now. The pastor realizes why he's the only one who's frustrated at the slowing growth rate.

Vision

Now, what's the common theme? Vision. In each case there's a dream of what a church should be. Crown Hills' layman dreams of beautiful buildings. Parkwood's pastor dreams of new members. Both Old First and Central dream of a community without the other. South Heights' frustrated pastor dreams of growth which seems unnecessary to his parishioners. Vision gives a church or minister a unique personality. As the Bible wisely says, "As [a man] thinketh in his heart, so is he" (Prov. 23:7).

Not all church dreams are created equal, of course. Some congregations are founded on hope and concern for others. Other congregations begin negative, contentious, or narrow in ministry and doctrine. A congregation's original dream shapes its future to a large extent.

Vision shapes future

The Size of Your Dream

A healthy church lives out of a healthy dream. For example, the *size* of a dream is crucial. What we expect from life is usually what we get. In *Winnie-the-Pooh*, Pooh and Piglet take an evening walk. For a long time they walk in companionable silence.

Finally, Piglet breaks the silence and asks, "When you wake up in the morning, Pooh, what's the first thing you say to yourself?"

"What's for breakfast?" answers Pooh. "And what do you say, Piglet?"

"I say, I wonder what exciting thing is going to happen today?"

Small expectations yield meager results. Unhealthy visions produce sick congregations. A church can choose a "breakfast dream" or an "excitement dream." Is it time for your church to examine its vision for either "breakfast" or "excitement"? Is your church ready to dream again?

Dreaming a Possible Dream

Dreams have impact. You can dream people into becoming! That's what Don Quixote did; his dreams for people helped them develop into what he dreamed.[1] For weeks after I'd seen *The Man of La Mancha* on stage, the lyric "To dream the impossible dream" lilted through my mind. Was Don Quixote the maddest man to dream impossible dreams? Or was he the sanest of men to sense the renewing power of a dream? I feel it was the latter. Don Quixote understood the "Pygmalion effect"; he knew expectations often come to life.

Persons and organizations are largely explained by their dreams. Over eighty times in the Gospels, Jesus spoke of his dream of the "kingdom of God." Jesus dreamed of a kingdom where God ruled redemptively in persons and over their institutions. This "kingdom dream" explains the words and works of Jesus.[2]

Jesus' dream clearly asks the pivotal question for any congregation: What is our ministry, our kingdom dream? And the general answer? Our ministry is to be the redeemed and redeeming people of God, to become the kingdom dream in local communities. No church can minister effectively until it identifies its unique ministry dream, a possible dream, and lives it out!

The local embodiments of the kingdom dream are virtually endless. Every church, like every person, has its own personality. A church shaped by its dream utilizes its spiritual and physical resources, develops its own history, and responds to its community environment in a unique manner. The best way to understand a church or organization is to discover its founding dream and any remnants of that original dream which continue to shape life and ministry.

Anatomy of a Congregation

Think of how you begin to understand a person. Likely you observe behavior, gather information about goals and values to clarify your impressions, and make some guesses about who this person is deep inside.

The same process helps you understand an organization. How does your church act? What does your congregation believe? Are those beliefs based on its dream? Does your church possess a dream? If so, is this vision commonly known and deeply held by the membership at large? These questions suggest a picture of organizational life.

Organizations move through a cycle of birth, growth, maturity, decline, and death.[3]

This cycle depicts the dynamic nature of organizational life. Every church is in the process of constant change as new ministers, different lay leaders, unique community circumstances, and fresh ministry opportunities arise. Churches can develop wholesomely out of their dream. Or, they can decline toward their organizational death.

The organizational health cycle can be described briefly. A healthy church is born out of a dream. A group of persons dream of a redemptive ministry in a community. They sense and share what they feel God wants from them in their setting at that moment. Then they take ownership of their vision, band together, and organizational life begins. They clarify their beliefs by Bible study, doctrinal statements, and the hymns they sing repeatedly. They set goals and priorities. They develop programs, policies and procedures, budgets, and institutional habits called norms. Finally, they minister out of the focused dream and the trust that has developed within the congregation.

Then, if the congregation doesn't take steps to open itself to revitalization, a plateau occurs. Decline begins. First, people doubt the structures. "It isn't working as well as it used to, is it?" they ask nostalgically. Next, they doubt the goals. "Is this the right way to work and minister?" Then, they doubt the organization's basic beliefs and assert, "This idea is wrong!" Finally, they become completely alienated and drop out in total disillusionment. This is absolute doubt and marks the death of the kingdom dream in these persons.

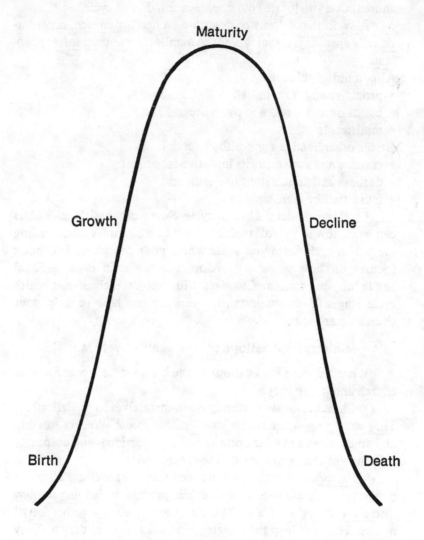

Maturity

Growth

Decline

Birth

Death

Picture the organizational life of an institution like your church. Can you locate your congregation on this cycle?

A "shorthand" way of describing a healthy church, organizationally speaking, is that it *plans.* An unhealthy church *solves* problems.

Also, a healthy church is . . .

- proactive and takes initiative for its ministry,
- builds on and is renewed by its dream, and
- ministers to others.

On the other hand, an unhealthy church is . . .

- reactive and surrenders its initiative for ministry,
- declines and doubts itself to death, and
- must itself be ministered to.

I call this model the health cycle. Savvy organizational leaders can learn how to "read" their congregation's health cycle. Reading the health cycle helps you sense where your church is. This book focuses on how you can develop and maintain organizational health in your church. Chapters will explore each of the health cycle stages. Most importantly, you'll learn how to help your church dream again!

Ministry Implications of the Health Cycle Model

What are some implications of the health cycle model for your church and its ministry?

Churches must constantly open themselves to revitalization. They must dream again! To stand still is to die. Weekly worship and study offer a regular opportunity for individual and corporate refreshment and refocusing on the dream.

Pastors help congregations keep their dream clear. They can nudge their organization into healthier practice by helping set new "here's who we are" and "here's how we work together best" norms. They will help the congregation plan from its dream. They will help build morale by focusing on the energy and hope generated by a new vision of the dream.

Dreaming churches plan; doubting churches solve problems.

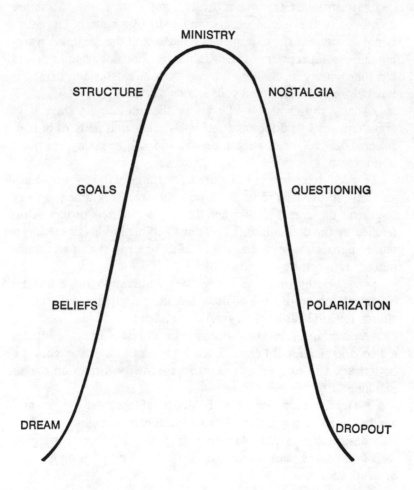

Regular cycles of personal, annual, and long-range planning, building off the dream, keep both the roots and directions of the church evident to its members.

• Restructure from your dreams, not your doubts. Structure grows out of the dream, beliefs, and goals of a church. Organizational structures exist to implement and extend the dream. A warning may be appropriate for new ministers. The honeymoon period is a time when restructuring is easier than later. But don't restructure before you understand your church's dream!

• Any church that cycles below the questioning stage is in grave danger. It is doubting itself into decline and perhaps organizational death. Questioning is, organizationally speaking, the point of no return.

• A church needs to be committed primarily to its dream goals and only secondarily to its program structure. Programs too weak to extend the dream should be allowed to die; new programs refreshed by the dream must be planned. Re-dreaming is generally a more appropriate organizational health strategy than reprogramming or restructuring.

• A healthy dream is a necessary foundation for a healthy organization. Nothing less than a kingdom dream will turn a church toward healthy and aggressive ministry.

A planning cycle rooted firmly in the dream is an indispensable aid to organizational health. Each cycle renews and stretches the organization to new heights. Kingdom ministry thrives on dream planning.

• Organizations contain the seeds of their own lives and deaths. Even congregations founded on healthy dreams can drift into destructive patterns. When organizations become aware of their decline, they can decide to dream again. This decision is a life-or-death choice.

ABC's of Church Health

The health cycle model is an alphabet to use in reading your church like a book. It's a basic tool. After applying this model to

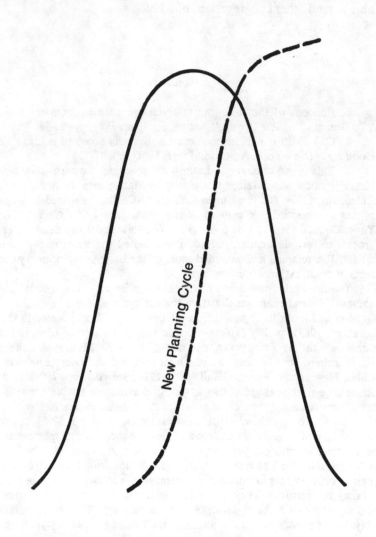

New Planning Cycle

your congregation by using the action exercises scattered throughout this book, you'll know your church much better. You'll also be
able to read other congregations quickly.

Notes

1. Portions of the following material are adapted from my article
"To Dream a Possible Dream," *Search,* Summer, 1978, pp. 35-38.
2. C. L. Mitton makes this almost universally accepted point in *The
Good News* (New York: Abingdon Press, 1961), pp. 71-79.
3. This *provolutionary* (a Latin word meaning "to turn toward the
future") model was developed originally by Management Designs, Inc. of
Cincinnati, Ohio, for the United Church of Christ. Published in a consultant's resource book entitled *Strengthening the Local Church* (New
York: Council for Lay Life & Work, 1974), this model was designed as a
process to revitalize congregations. I've adapted the terms in the initial
model; I've retained and extended most of the basic provolutionary con-
cepts of organizational life, however.

The life cycle format has often been applied to organizational phenomena. Several examples illustrate the life cycle school of thought: (1)
Gordon L. Lippitt in *Organizational Renewal* (New York: Meredith Corporation, 1969), p. 29, depicts the "developmental stages of organizational growth" as birth, youth, and maturity. (2) Paul Hersey & Kenneth
H. Blanchard in *Management of Organizational Behavior* (Englewood
Cliffs, New Jersey: Prentice-Hall, Inc., 1977, 3rd ed.), pp. 299-302, describe organizational growth as a series of evolution (stable growth)—
revolution (crisis) stages. (3) E. Mansel Pattison in *Pastor & Parish—a
Systems Approach* (Philadelphia: Fortress Press, 1977), pp. 57-69, applies
developmental stages to the church and claims a social system matures as it
moves from storming to forming to norming to performing. (4) The Louis
A. Allen Associates, an international business consulting firm, advertise in
their brochures that companies experience an adolescent stage between
infancy and maturity. They term this crucial stage "the corridor of crisis"
and depict it as a make-or-break organizational stage. They note, remark-
ably, of the twenty largest companies in the United States forty years ago,
only *two* are still among the first twenty in size. Of the one hundred largest
companies twenty-five years ago, *almost half* have disappeared or have

declined substantially from their peak. Further information on the management system the Allen Associates has developed is available from 615 University Avenue, Palo Alto, CA 94301. (5) David O. Moberg in *The Church as a Social Institution* (Englewood Cliffs, New Jersey: Prentice-Hall, Inc., 1962), pp. 118-124, applies a life cycle approach to denominations.

2
Ingredients for Church Health

Bethel Church had been in conflict. The search for a new pastor had begun the healing process. Overall, however, the congregation's ministry was still in disarray. The new minister carefully sized up the church situation and called a meeting of the congregation's leaders.

Tenderly he acknowledged their pain. The pastor also leveled with them about low morale and uneven participation. Then, he dared them to dream with him about what Bethel could become. Over a hundred specific ministry ideas grew out of this meeting and other conversations which followed.

So many possibilities were before Bethel that her defeatism disappeared. The mainstream ideas were clustered around themes and developed into a three-year plan. Attendance doubled and giving tripled within six months.

Neighboring congregations admire Bethel's external success. What observers see less frequently is the organizational ability of Bethel's new pastor and leader corps. They have developed three ingredients for church health at Bethel. First, they understand what kind of organization Bethel is. They appreciate some new roles their pastor can provide. And they are working out a theological vision of the visible church.

What Kind of Organization?

A church is a special organization. From an organizational perspective, what are the distinctive qualities of a church? What

22

roles do congregations play as organizations?

The church is a *mission-oriented organization*. Each church has a mission. It exists to extend the kingdom of God—the redemptive dream of Jesus. The church calls persons to live by distinctly Christian values, to incarnate Jesus' kingdom dream. This is the prophetic role of the church.

The church is a *service organization*. Congregations assume a servant role. A constant tension faced by any church is to balance service (external ministry) and "serve-us" (internal ministry). As a not-for-profit institution, the church literally gives itself away through concrete ministry. Sacrificial service is the priestly role of the church.

The church is a *modeling organization*. Mind molding is the challenge that's always before any group hoping to exercise cultural, social, and value influence. The church incarnates a new model, the Christ life. Congregations plan to shape the lives and consciences of their own members and other persons who reside in their community. The church can afford to risk to shape the future because its ultimate future is secure. Modeling is the kingly role of the church.

The church is a *volunteer organization.* To be effective, volunteer groups must ask and answer satisfactorily four basic questions. These key questions define the participative role of the church.

• What is our mission? is the most fundamental question a volunteer organization can ask itself.[1] Religious organizations must be extra sharp in defining their reason(s) for existing. Businesses can say, "Our purpose is to make a profit," or "We exist to sell one warehouse full of widgets every month." The church, however, deals in relationships—relationships of persons to God and persons to other persons. These relational matters are much more difficult to see and measure. Consequently, congregations often define their mission in vague generalities or not at all.

• What does our church pay its volunteers? is another crucial question.[2] Volunteers at work together create a very special style of organization. There are no paychecks or fringe benefits for volunteers. However, volunteers are "paid" in spiritual or psychological gains. Everyone gets something—Christian service, recognition, new learning, a channel for energy, a moral way to fill time and structure life—for one's time and money, or one probably would not contribute one's energy. Therefore, congregations must become very clear about the benefits they extend to their volunteers.

3. • How are we unique in a world already crowded with other volunteer organizations? is a difficult issue to confront. Congregations usually have more competition than they suspect. For instance, a rural community in eastern North Carolina with 1,100 residents counted its volunteer organizations. It discovered 83 formally organized groups, including 7 churches. That's 75 volunteer organizations for every 1,000 population! When informed of these statistics, a longtime resident replied, "I thought it would be closer to a thousand. It sometimes seems we have more organizations than people around here."[3]

Churches, as volunteer organizations, are in competition with such organizations as 4-H, Girl Scouts, Weight Watchers, and the PTA for people's time. Therefore, congregations have to consider how much time and allegiance they can expect and will demand from members. Religiously, God demands all. Organizationally, the church often must settle for less.

4. • Is our church healthy? is the final question. Volunteer organizations are the most complex and sophisticated organizational form known. Volunteer organizations don't coerce their members. Persons join for motivations other than wages. These characteristics make volunteer groups challenging to understand and lead. Since there are only two organizational climates possible—healthy and unhealthy—it's paramount that congregations develop and maintain organizational health. The health cycle model lends church leaders a concrete method to use in understanding some key issues in organizational health.

The Ministry of Congregational Health

Ministers have a key role in church health. Ministers already wear many hats. They traditionally have preached, taught, led worship, and done evangelism. Developing roles are pastoral care, counseling, family enrichment, and grief ministry. The newest roles to emerge in pastoral ministries are leadership, management, and organization development.

The ministry of congregational health calls on church leaders to nourish the body of Christ. Organizational development in the church places some new, but necessary, roles upon the minister and church lay leaders.

• Minister as Congregational Consultant—The minister can guide the congregation toward health as an internal consultant. This crucial helping ministry enables the congregation to discover its unique personality, limitations, and opportunities. The minister can design and facilitate processes that define the kingdom dream and move the body of believers toward health.[4]

Specifically, the action exercises in this book provide clue questions and frameworks for developing a complete profile of congregational health. The information you gather through the action exercises will give you a reading on your church.

• Minister as Church Diagnostician—"Reading" congregations is a crucial ministry skill.[5] The health cycle model offers a structure for congregational analysis, diagnosis, and revitalization. By using this model, leaders can discover which stage their churches are in, isolate key issues, and intervene constructively to trigger health and renewal.

For example, let's assume your congregation is in the nostalgia stage. That's your discovery through analysis. What do you do, then, to awaken new vitality in the total organization?

(a) Look directly across the model for the sticking point. Nostalgia is doubting structure; this diagnosis pinpoints the trouble spot as structure. A common mistake at this point is simply to restructure. But that's generally too cosmetic and helps only briefly.

(b) Since structure grows out of the organization's goals, the cure is usually found in an examination of the goals. Do the goals and structure mesh? Have new or different goals left the structure largely outmoded?

(c) Preventive organizational medicine is in returning to a

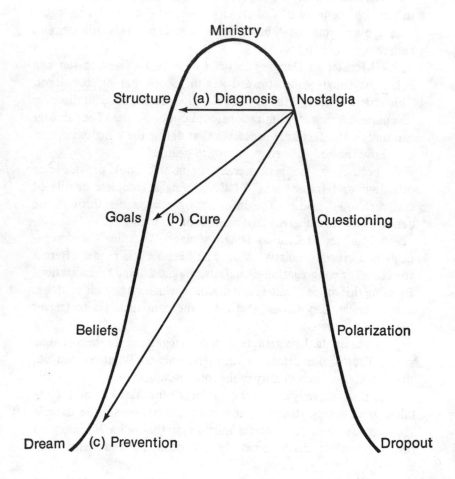

Ministry

Structure ← (a) Diagnosis — Nostalgia

Goals ← (b) Cure — Questioning

Beliefs — Polarization

Dream ← (c) Prevention — Dropout

sharpened, owned, and communicated kingdom dream. The dream contains the spiritual and emotional motivation to launch a congregation on a new cycle of redemptive ministry.

• Minister as Growth Planner—Ministers can become visionary managers. Visionary—unleashing the prophetic energy and sense of group power in the dream. Manager—using resources wisely. One skill blends together the art of the visionary and the science of resource management: planning. Any minister who hopes to be effective as a leader and growth agent will develop planning as the vehicle for congregational effectiveness. If the kingdom dream is the launchpad for church health, planning from the dream is the rocket to healthy growth.

Seeds for a Theology of Congregational Health

A major ingredient is still missing in applying organizational health techniques to congregations. We have no explicit theology of the visible church.[6] We have primarily a methodology for life in the visible congregation as prescribed by our denominations.

Historically, theologians have spoken more of the mystical "bride of Christ" than the visible "body of Christ." The invisible, supernatural aspects of formal ecclesiology have been spelled out more fully than a theology for the gathered fellowship on mission in the world. Protestant thinkers have spoken of the visible church to some degree. For example, Karl Barth asserts, "The first congregation was a visible group, which caused a visible public uproar. If the Church has not this visibility, then it is not the Church."[7]

In the Corinthian letter, Paul described the "body of Christ" in tangible terms. Christ's body is visible, diverse, unified, and interdependent (1 Cor. 12:12-31). These images provide a fertile seedbed in which to plant a new theology, a theology of the social system we call the church. Systemic theology provides a budding theology for the visible church.

Using Paul's "body of Christ" idea as the shaping metaphor, a systemic theology for the visible church develops further in the pastoral letters. Systemic theology focuses on

*the church of extended duration rather than the church of the
imminent return. It is the church with a ministry to its members and a mission to its age rather than a church which
simply waits for its Lord to return. It is a church with polity,
politics, prayer and program. It has a purpose for its being
and a plan for its life.[8]

It is this church for which we've developed more methodology than
theology until now. Appendix A at the end of the book outlines
some assumptions of systemic theology in more detail.

Where to from Here?

Too often we in the church have been told what to do to develop successful programs. Less often have we been told why we
Christians minister to others. This book focuses on why we dream
of God's redemption and how to develop healthy congregations.

To our earlier model of congregational health, stir in the three
ingredients related to organizational types, minister roles, and
systemic theology. Using these foundations, let's look in detail at
the process of triggering congregational health by dreaming again.

Notes

1. Peter Drucker, *Management: Tasks, Responsibilities, Practices*
(New York: Harper & Row, Publishers, 1974), pp. 74-94. While this
chapter focuses on "business purpose and business mission," the issue is
so basic to organizational health and effectiveness that church leaders
would do well to apply this concept to congregational life.

2. Lyle E. Schaller, *The Pastor and the People* (Nashville: Abingdon
Press, 1973), pp. 80-86.

3. Lyle E. Schaller, *Understanding Tomorrow* (Nashville: Abingdon
Press, 1976), pp. 96-97.

4. A number of fine resources is available to help ministers understand the consultant role and build consultant skills. For stimulating reading, see Edgar H. Schein, *Process Consultation* (Reading, Massachusetts:

Addison-Wesley Publishing Co., Inc., 1969); Robert R. Blake and Jane Srygley Mouton, *Consultation* (Reading, Massachusetts: Addison-Wesley Publishing Co., Inc., 1976); and Walter H. Mahler, *Diagnostic Studies* (Reading, Massachusetts: Addison-Wesley Publishing Co., Inc., 1974).

5. For some approaches to organizational diagnosis, see Seymour L. Rosenberg, *Self-Analysis of Your Organization* (New York: AMACOM, 1974); Jack K. Fordyce and Raymond Weil, *Managing with People* (Reading, Massachusetts: Addison-Wesley Publishing Co., Inc., 1971); Walter R. Mahler, *Diagnostic Studies* (Reading, Massachusetts: Addison-Wesley Publishing Co., Inc., 1974); and Marvin R. Weisbord,, "Organizational Diagnosis: Six Places to Look for Trouble with or without a Theory" in *Group and Organization Studies*, Vol. No. 4, December, 1976, pp. 430-447.

6. Thomas C. Oden, *Beyond Revolution* (Philadelphia: Westminster Press, 1970), p. 53.

7. Karl Barth, *Dogmatics in Outline* (New York: Harper & Row, Publishers, 1959), p. 142.

8. H. Newton Malony, "Toward a Theology for Organization Development," *Christian Ministry*, July, 1975, p. 20.

Part II
The Healthy Congregation

3
Christ's Kingdom—
A Possible Dream!

Langston Hughes, the black poet, has grasped the power of a life vision: "Hold fast to dreams, for if dreams die, life is a broken winged bird that cannot fly." Churches are birthed out of a dream.

Where does a redemptive vision come from? Two sources come to mind immediately—from my and others' vision of redemption and from biblical teachings. In fact, in the church, these two sources often flow together into a personal and congregational dream.

Inventory Your Dream!

We who minister help our churches dream their dreams. Therefore, we too must live out of a clear personal dream.

Arthur Miller's *Death of a Salesman* depicts the cost of a wrong dream. Willie Loman was a born craftsman; he could have become a skilled cabinetmaker. His gifted hands had fashioned the front stoop of his house. But Willie tried instead to become a supersalesman. When his sales dropped, he snapped under the strain and killed himself. Biff, Willie's son, stood by his father's grave and said, "There's more of him in that front stoop than in all the sales he ever made. He had the wrong dreams. All, all wrong."[1]

Jesus had a dream of God's kingdom. He taught and lived his vision like most young men in their late twenties. Jesus' kingdom dream was the organizing and motivating fact in his life. Daniel

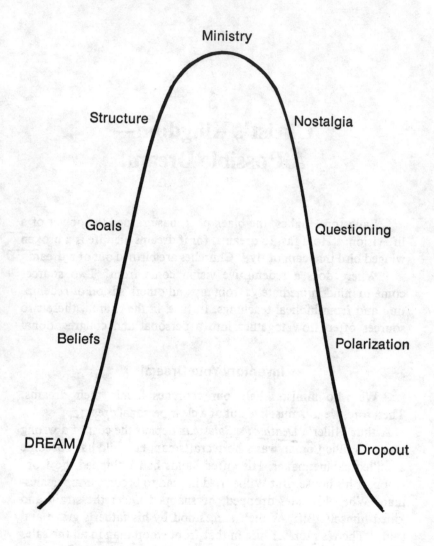

Ministry

Structure   Nostalgia

Goals   Questioning

Beliefs   Polarization

DREAM   Dropout

Levinson, after extensive study of American males' developmental patterns, says the dream in young adults is "more formed than pure fantasy, yet less articulated than a fully thought-out plan." Furthermore, the dream "has the quality of a vision, an imagined possibility that generates excitement and vitality."[2] To understand and follow Jesus, we must understand his dream of the kingdom of God.

The first step in awakening a kingdom dream in a congregation is for the minister and key leaders to share a vision of the church. Why? Because a personal dream often blooms into a corporate dream. As Emerson said, "An institution is but the lengthened shadow of a man."

Before you use the following checklist and the other action exercises that appear throughout this book, let me suggest several ways you can use these exercises:

(1) Reflect by yourself through the clue questions that follow. Use your own knowledge and impressions of your congregation to deepen and broaden your individual perspective.

(2) Talk to others informally, using the clue questions as a casual basis for developing further your view of your church.

(3) Enlist a formal consultant team of church members. This should be a varied group representing females and males, a span of ages, and different lengths of membership and levels of activity. A long-range planning committee or church council may give you an existing group to work with.

ACTION EXERCISE #1

Personal Ministry Inventory

What is your dream for your own ministry? The minister must imagine, sense opportunities, locate real needs, make calculated guesses about the future's possibilities, put ideas into practical plans, and call persons to kingdom service. Ministers must be visionary managers of congregational resources.

Here's a ladder-like checklist for outlining a visionary ministry for yourself:

• What *kind of Christians* do I dream of?

• What *kind of church program* must I develop to grow my dream Christians?

• What *kind of leadership team* of volunteer and/ or paid staff must I develop to produce my dream church program?

• What *kind of minister* must I become to gather my dream leadership team?

• What *kind of support system* of family, peers, and friends do I need to help me become the minister I dream of? In the words of the sage, "Where there is no vision, the people perish" (Prov. 29:18). But where there's a kingdom dream, God's people flourish.

People's dreams define their lives to a large extent. William Herbert Carruth's poem, "Dreamer of Dreams," shows how the rise and fall of personal dreams shape our lives.[3]

We are all of us dreamers of dreams,
    On visions our childhood is fed;
And the heart of the child is unhaunted, it seems,
    By the ghosts of dreams that are dead.

From childhood to youth's but a span
    And the years of our life are soon sped;
But the youth is no longer a youth, but a man,
    When the first of his dreams is dead.

. . . .

He may live on by compact and plan
    When the fine bloom of living is shed,
But God pity the little that's left of a man
    When the last of his dreams is dead.

> Let him show a brave face if he can,
> Let him woo fame or fortune instead,
> Yet there's not much to do but to bury a man
> When the last of his dreams is dead.

Without a dream a person has no direction in life. A dream gives a person a story to tell.

Organizations dream too. They are launched out of their members' vision of life. Two experts on developing organizations note that "at its inception, any organization is an expression of the purposes of its individual founders."[4] So organizations develop their stories and tell them over and over again. The organization transmits its story to all who will listen.

Retelling Kingdom Stories

Jesus came telling stories. His primary teaching method was parable telling. Many of the parables begin, "The kingdom of God is like . . ." These kingdom stories are variously numbered at 50 to 60 and make up about 35 percent of Jesus' teachings.[5] Over 80 times in the Gospels Jesus spoke of the kingdom of God. Virtually all of his parables centered on the kingdom vision.

The kingdom stories of Jesus relate to awakening congregational dreams in three crucial dimensions.

• Kingdom stories are easy to communicate. They are narratives that are part of our common vocabulary. For example, when a person becomes an obvious sinner, he is often described as a "prodigal" (Luke 15:11-24).

Parables are word-pictures. They compare and contrast the full range of life experience. Some kingdom stories are one-frame cartoons and take a proverb-like form (Mark 3:24). Other kingdom stories resemble short films; they tell brief stories like the good Samaritan (Luke 10:25-37). The *communication factor* helps visionary ministers express a redemptive dream through retelling Jesus' kingdom stories.

• Kingdom stories make learning exciting. The *educational factor* of the parables indicates their capacity to stimulate thinking.

They act like reflectors that focus light on their subjects. Each parable concentrates on a single truth about the kingdom.

3. • Kingdom stories are picturesque and vivid. Parables engage our imaginations. Their impact and involvement turn our ears into eyes and help us "see" what we hear. The kingdom stories are so unforgettable they are considered the purest form of Jesus' teaching we have. We are drawn to Jesus' parables and act on them because they trigger insight and action. The kingdom stories contain a motivation factor that energizes persons to respond to the kingdom dream.

Jesus' kingdom stories make his kingdom dream concrete. Healthy congregations dream of a visible kingdom and work to organize and live out their dreams. Then, they tell and retell their stories. A sermon or teaching series on the parables is a productive way to help church members begin considering a kingdom dream for themselves.

Kingdom Dream Themes

I can't define a kingdom dream for your particular congregation. I don't know the special needs and ministry opportunities of your congregation and community. But I sense there are some foundational themes that provide bases for unique congregational expressions of the kingdom of God.

A kingdom dream begins with redemption. God's consistent purpose has always been to redeem his creatures and creation. Redemption is the Bible's story in a single word.

The parables strongly extend the theme of redemptive grace. The two debtors (Luke 7:36-50), the lost sheep and lost coin (Luke 15:1-10), the waiting father, better known as the prodigal son (Luke 15:11-32), and the unforgiving debtor (Matt. 18:23-35) all tell of God's mercy toward sinners. Repenting and believing are fitting actions for persons who give themselves to God's kingdom.

Redeeming persons and their institutions is basic kingdom ministry. Congregations must dream and work for God's redemption in the world. Without redemption as its baseline, a church can become a social club or a short-term helping agency. Redemption is always the bottom line of a kingdom dream.

A kingdom dream envisions *God ruling.* Obedience is the response of a subject to his king. The highest value of his daily life becomes the kingdom of God.

Again, the parables speak of the dynamic of sacrificing for kingdom participation. God rules actively and continuously; the kingdom citizen responds readily and joyfully. The tower builder and the warring king (Luke 14:28-33), the hidden treasure and precious pearl (Matt. 13:44-46), the unresponsive neighbor and the callous judge (Luke 11:5-8; 18:2-8), the farmer and his helper (Luke 17:7-10), the two builders (Matt. 7:24-27) all call on men and women of the kingdom to hear God's ruling commands and to do his bidding.

To do the will of God is the individual Christian's highest goal. The kingdom of God demands a corporate commitment to God's will. Congregations must seek and pledge themselves to act as a body on the instructions of a ruling God. A Christ-centered, positive ministry approach reflects a kingdom dream in a church.

A kingdom dream makes Christ *concrete.* Jesus incarnated the kingdom of God. Jesus acted out some of his parables, as well as telling many others. The triumphal entry, cleansing of the Temple, and the Lord's Supper are enacted or embodied parables.

Jesus came preaching the gospel of the kingdom. His message was neither pie in the sky by-and-by nor abstract theory. Jesus lived the kingdom concretely. Christian disciples and congregations are called to incarnate the kingdom of God in every generation. A kingdom dream becomes tangible in a congregation's ministry.

A kingdom dream triggers *growth* and change. The kingdom changes people and their institutions. The theme of growth runs throughout the parables. The sower (Mark 4:3-8), the seed growing secretly (Mark 4:26-29), the mustard seed and leaven (Luke 13:18-21; Mark 4:30-32), the weeds among the wheat (Matt. 13:24-30), and the kernel of wheat (John 12:24) make growth and change a constant in the kingdom. For a person or congregation to develop a kingdom dream means willingly accepting the risks of growing and changing their early hopes.

Discovering Founding Dreams

What was the original dream of your congregation? Unearthing the dream your church was founded upon may take some careful analysis and imagination. If many years have elapsed and long-time members aren't available or poor records have been kept, you may not be able to discover accurately your church's founding dream. However, the originating dream is likely woven into the past history and current behavior patterns of your congregation.

Some facets of the dream will be obvious. For example, after a bitter division in the Without Spot or Blemish Church, some dissident members withdrew and established a rival church across the street. They named it the Greater Without Spot or Blemish Church! The name tells the tale.

Transactional analysis, an approach to social psychiatry, has demonstrated our lives have an element of predictability—as if they are lived out of a playwright's script. Script analysis can help an individual understand and cope with some of the predictable patterns of his life.

Organizations have scripts too.[6] Your church has been scripted to behave by its dream, history, and decisions. Past patterns may be more deeply entrenched than you have seen or believed before. Persons and churches quickly become creatures of habit.

A favorite story of mine relates to the gold rush days of 1849. As the numerous wagon trains left Saint Joseph, Missouri, for the trek across the prairies already rutted by the tracks of earlier wagons, their eager occupants read this sobering message on a banner across the western end of the main street: "Choose your rut carefully. You may be in it all the way to California!" Discovering your church's script will help you understand and minister better—even if you find some ruts that run almost from coast to coast.

The following informal script questionnaire can help you diagnose your church's predictable patterns and challenge and change some routines that run counter to a kingdom dream. With the aid of this questionnaire, some historical information, and analytical observation of your church's current behavior, you can clarify the scripted dream of your congregation.

ACTION EXERCISE #2

A Script Questionnaire for a Church

ACT I: The Early Days

1. Who was our church's founder? Its first pastor? The charter members? How would I describe these persons?
2. How was our church born? Out of positive or negative circumstances?
3. What do the earliest records of our church say about our church's beginning?
4. What projects were undertaken first by our church?
5. Does our church constitution, bylaws, or legal documents contain any unique or unusual features? Do they speak for or against certain themes which indicate early issues?
6. Are there any memorial areas or items in our church? What are they? Under what circumstances were they given and/or dedicated?
7. What are the favorite stories and most unforgettable events of the early years?
8. How was our church's name selected?

ACT II: The Golden Years

1. What were the greatest growth period(s) of our church?
2. Who were the pastor(s) then? For how long?
3. What were those pastors' slogans and mottoes?
4. Who were the key laypersons during the greatest

growth period(s)? What did they represent?

5. What projects and new programs were initiated during these growth periods?

6. What have been the issues and problems over which people have conflicted regularly in our church?

7. When were buildings erected? What do these projects represent?

8. Which events and persons from this era are "magic" and are still remembered and discussed? Why?

ACT III: The Present Moment

1. Who gets recognition in our church? For what?

2. What priorities does our church budget point to?

3. How does our church now reflect its beginnings? How is our church different from its founding dream?

4. What is the prevailing feeling tone of our church? Fellowship and love? Guilt, fear, or anger? Service?

5. What forces keep our church as it is? What or who are the traditionalizing forces?

6. What are the special celebrations of our church?

7. If our church were one person, who would it be?

Do you have a clearer idea of your church's founding dream now? Is it a kingdom dream? Or, is it perhaps a lesser dream? If it is an unhealthy dream, do you want to help your congregation rewrite its script and develop a new life plan?

Churches, like persons, have three choices about their scripts. (1) They can *live* their scripts, whether healthy or unhealthy. (2) They can try to *avoid* their scripts, if they are unhealthy. (3) They can rewrite their scripts, *changing* them from unhealthy to healthy. Rewriting demands an awareness of the destructive pattern of the old script and a congregational choice to end the old and commit themselves to a new script reflecting a kingdom dream. A new vision of the ministry your church can develop is the surest route to a healthy ministry and a story worth telling.

Redemptive Dream as Story Management

Life stories shape our dreams. As a boy, I read hero stories— mostly sports and frontier tales. Jim Thorpe, Babe Ruth, Mickey Mantle, Joe Louis, the Lone Ranger, Daniel Boone, Davy Crockett, and Jim Bowie were some personal favorites. Little did I know, or care, that these stories were somewhat romanticized. I needed these models to imitate. I needed some dreams to live out. Each of us needs our story to tell. For that reason *Roots* became a national event—a folk event.

Hero stories and folklore are vehicles for understanding and transmitting our heritage. These stories describe how we got this way. They tell personal stories and express truths profoundly. Putting life experience in story form makes abstract principles concrete and universal, like Jesus' parables.

A congregation is full of "clue stories." These stories tell "the truth in symbolic clothing."[7] They explain our churches to us. Clue stories have several specific functions.

(1) Clue stories have a religious function. They depict our sense of awe at the mystery of life. For example, the Indians of the American plains thought the Great Spirit lived in the Black Hills. After seeing the beauty of those hills, I can understand better why the Indians felt the Black Hills would be a suitable home for God. Furthermore, when the Hebrews wanted to tell of God's love and redeeming actions, they didn't philosophize. They rehearsed Egypt and the Exodus. These events recounted their corporate experiences with the God who had loved and redeemed them.

(2) Clue stories may also have a scientific function. They give us a picture of our universe. For instance, during the 1906 San Francisco earthquake many residents of Chinatown tried to drive a bull from the streets. These Chinese believed the universe was supported at its corners by four bulls. They reasoned the bull they were driving had abandoned his post and caused the quake. Their efforts further terrified and enraged the bull. A policeman finally killed the bull. That action must have frightened the Chinese terribly

since they no longer saw any hope of repairing the universe.

(3) Clue stories can serve a cultural function too. They support our social order and mold new generations. Ethnic festivals, crafts fairs, and art and history museums help explain how our society has developed.

(4) Finally, clue stories have a psychological function. They guide us through life's passages. Stories describe the emotional impact of adolescent rebellion, becoming a parent, and aging and retirement.

Clue stories grow up around the history of a congregation.[8] Outstanding events become the "campfire stories" of a church and describe key persons and events which have shaped the congregation's life. One country church I know about is located by a clear spring. Community leaders claim the spring originated years ago when a slave woman and her children were dying of thirst during a drought. In despair of finding water, the slave woman prayed. Then she found the spring. Even during the longest droughts this spring has never dried up. The community members interpret the spring as a sign of the presence and provision of God. Interestingly enough, this congregation has never had a major conflict involving the entire congregation during its nearly two hundred years of service. I suspect their story of God's constant care has helped keep their history healthy.

A kingdom dream has an epic quality about it. Participating in God's kingdom is a fact so comprehensive and a truth so majestic we constantly struggle to define and communicate it. This profound story is the thrust of the mission of the church. Christians' spirits and imaginations long for a story profound enough to tell and retell—even if our words and lives are too small to fully capture the power of God's ruling love.

Dreaming or Drifting

A congregation's dream must be clearly known by its members. Yet a statement of a kingdom dream is rarely encompassed adequately by a few words. God's purpose of redemption is always greater than our imaginations, hopes, and vocabularies. But our continuing witness in word and life is our best vehicle for telling his story.

Stating and publicizing your congregation's dream is critical. Either the sharp focus of your congregation's resources of people, facilities, money, energy, and information is on a defined dream or your church is using its resources ineffectively to some degree.

Drift begins early in organizations. Even if the early dream was potent and public, it is the nature of organizations to dull their focus and drift. Any congregation that's attempting ministry without clear reference to its dream is drifting. Goals are generalizations and are, therefore, hard to keep sharply defined and publicly stated. The loss of a sense of direction is the most profound problem a congregation must face as an organization.[9]

Several strategies help anchor drift.

• Put your dream into a plan. Becoming proactive and taking initiative stymies drift.

• Use all resources now. Be sure members who are not fully involved are included in the congregation's planning and ministry.

• Focus on needs. Leaders are often tempted to reorganize to halt drift. Congregations which meet needs direct resources toward persons primarily, not structure.

A full range of strategies for helping a congregation shape its kingdom dream appears in chapter 10. For now, try to define the fundamental direction of your congregation through the following action exercise's clue questions.

ACTION EXERCISE #3

What Is the Foundational Aim of Our Church?

I. Basic Identity
    Who are we? Do we have a ministry dream? Where are we as an organization? Are we on the planning incline

or problem-solving decline of the organizational health cycle?

II. Unique Contribution

What is our unique contribution in our community? What is the special strength of our congregation? What is the distinctive nature of our ministry?

III. Primary Audience

Who is our primary audience? Are our programs, finances, and energies focused primarily toward our church family or beyond our church? Does our ministry tend to select particular age, social, economic, or educational groups? Which new audience(s) will we try to reach?

IV. Resource Use

How do we use our basic resources: people, money, time, information, and physical facilities? Which resource do we value most? Least?

V.   Strategic Game Plan

How will we multiply our membership growth rate? How will we train our people for ministry? How will we influence our community? How will we expand our stewardship potential? How will we enrich our own fellowship?

Curing Tunnel Vision

Jesus stressed the kingdom rather than the church by a ratio of forty to one. The church is an organizational expression of the kingdom of God. Some congregations may suffer from methological tunnel vision by majoring on their church and minoring on the kingdom. These groups may ask too often, "How can we 'do church' here?" to the near exclusion of "How can we bring God's kingdom through this congregation?" A kingdom dream will undergird our methods with a theology big enough to cure tunnel vision.

Keep in mind that a dream always comes first. A leadership expert notes:

Not much happens without a dream. And for something great to happen there must be a great dream. Behind every great achievement is a dreamer of great dreams. Much more than a dreamer is required to bring it to reality; but the dream must be there first.[10]

Christ's kingdom is a possible dream for your church.

Notes

1. Arthur Miller, *Death of a Salesman* (New York: Viking Press, Inc., 1958), p. 138.

2. Daniel J. Levinson, et al., *The Seasons of a Man's Life* (New York: Alfred A. Knopf, 1978), p. 91.

3. William Herbert Carruth, "Dreamers of Dreams," in James D. Morrison's, *Masterpieces of Religious Verse* (New York: Harper & Brothers, 1948), p. 278.

4. Paul R. Lawrence and Jay W. Lorsch, *Developing Organizations* (Reading, Massachusetts: Addison-Wesley Publishing Co., Inc., 1969), pp. 6 and 15.

5. A. M. Hunter, *Interpreting the Parables* (Philadelphia: Westminster Press, 1960), p. 7. For additional perspectives on the parables as kingdom stories, see Joachim Jeremias, *The Parables of Jesus* (New York: Charles Scribner's Sons, 1955); A. M. Hunter, *The Parables Then and Now* (Philadelphia: Westminster Press, 1971); and Eugene S. Wehrli, *Exploring the Parables* (Boston: United Church Press, 1963).

6. Dorothy Jongeward, *Everybody Wins: Transactional Analysis Applied to Organizations* (Reading, Massachusetts: Addison-Wesley Publishing Co., Inc., 1973), pp. 5-31. For definitive treatments of personal scripts, see Claude M. Steiner, *Scripts People Live* (New York: Grove Press, 1974) and Eric Berne, *What Do You Say After You Say Hello?* (New York: Grove Press, 1972). A helpful exploration of the influence of folk tales on shaping life's meanings is Bruno Bettleheim's *The Uses of Enchantment* (New York: Alfred A. Knopf, 1976).

7. Joseph Campbell, *The Hero with a Thousand Faces* (Princeton,

48 TO DREAM AGAIN

New Jersey: Princeton University Press, 2nd ed., 1968), p. vii. For additional perspectives from Campbell, see "The Need for New Myths," *Time,* January 17, 1972, pp. 50-51. For a helpful discussion of our need to experience again the power and imagination of the biblical record, see Guilford Dudley III, *The Recovery of Christian Myth* (Philadelphia: Westminster Press, 1967).

8. For informative material on organizational clue stories, see Ian I. Mitroff and Ralph H. Kilmann, "Stories Managers Tell: A New Tool for Organizational Problem Solving," *Management Review,* July, 1975, p. 18 *ff* and Leland P. Bradford and Jerry B. Harvey, "Dealing with Dysfunctional Organization Myths" in Wyatt Warner Burke and Harvey A. Hornstein's *The Social Technology of Organization Development* (Fairfax, Virginia: Learning Resources Corporation, 1972), pp. 244-254.

9. Seymour L. Rosenberg, *Self-Analysis of Your Organization* (New York: AMACOM, 1974), p. 28.

10. Robert K. Greenleaf, *Servant Leadership* (New York: Paulist/ Newman Press, 1977), p. 16.

4
What Your Congregation Believes

My college roommate was a committed Christian. But like many church members, he didn't speak of his faith glibly. His theology wasn't yet refined or systematic.

One evening, while I was studying for an exam, another friend in the dormitory dropped by our room to chat. My roommate and the visitor somehow fell into a conversation about the hymnal. Before I realized what was happening, they began a loud and lusty duet—and then another and another.

At first I was aggravated that they were being so noisy at a time when I needed to study. Then I became curious and finally fascinated by what was happening. They would leaf through the hymnal for a few pages, spy a familiar hymn, pounce on it like a priceless treasure, and "testify" about it. Usually they'd say something like, "Grandma loved this one! I remember her singing this song while she baked cookies." Then they would raise the roof with the gusto of their singing. Whatever they lacked in harmony, they made up for in volume. Then they would return to the hymnal and repeat the scene again.

Several times during the hour or two they serenaded me they cried over a hymn. They would recall warm, personal experiences related to the hymn, and say, "I love this song! Why don't we sing it more often at church?" The depth of their emotion in the singing and discussing of their favorite hymns caught me off guard.

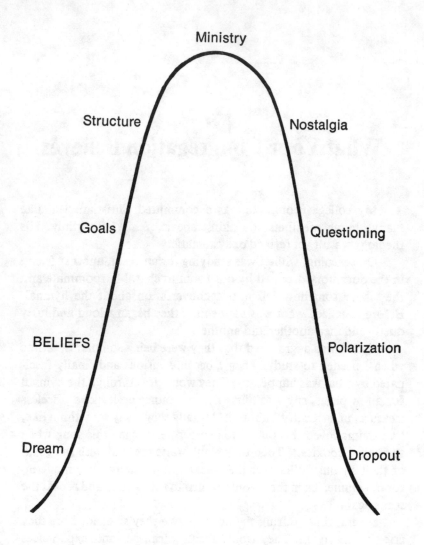

Ministry

Structure   Nostalgia

Goals   Questioning

BELIEFS   Polarization

Dream   Dropout

I became convinced this unusual display of religious fervor by two otherwise fun-loving college boys was very significant. They ordinarily wouldn't discuss their religious beliefs. But they could sing what they felt about Christ and his church. The doctrine they had absorbed in worship, Sunday School, and church camps overflowed into feelings as they sang. Given words by the hymn writer, these two university students expressed the important elements of their Christianity that evening.

Infected by Faith

C. S. Lewis once described the contagious joy and sharing of the gospel as infectious faith. He was correct. Christianity is much more likely to be caught than taught. Often our personal theology is not well organized or easily defined. We may not always be able to explain God, but we can tell the story of what God is doing in our lives. That's experiential theology—faith based on and understood out of our own pilgrimages.

A North Carolina fire chief commented on a church fire with an intensely personal dimension. "Watching a church building burn where you have received so many personal blessings and remembering others who have also received so many blessings was a very hard thing to do. That's where I learned to sing my first song—'Blessed Assurance'—page 269."[1] When this fireman remembered his past faith experiences, he recalled blessings and hymns of his congregation of fellow Christians.

Experiential theology is our personal faith story. We ask, What do I know about God? Does my life match my theology? The experiential theologian, then, is a person who knows his own journey, recognizes the plots of holy ground in his experience, and tells his story of God active in him. Experiential theology has four unique characteristics.

• Experiential theology is intuitive. It's more instinctual than deliberately planned. There's a sixth-sense quality about experiential theology. It knows without deliberate prior learning. It's knowledge at a subconscious level. Experiential theology knows the melody even without memorizing the words.

2- • Experiential theology is spontaneous. It's a contagion, wild and free, impulsive, emotional, and unrestrained. Experiential theology is energetic and taps the internal wellsprings of natural enthusiasm.

3- • Experiential theology is repetitious. Habit, pattern, and recurrence mark a theology of experience. Actions and values based on experiential theology are duplicated again and again without thought.

4- • Experiential theology has a corporate expression. This is probably the most crucial aspect of experiential theology. Corporate life is bound together by a subtle sense of belonging. A family-like atmosphere in a group creates trust, identity, and communion. Experiential theology is aware of the underground feelings that unite persons around a mutual vision.

I'm not describing a folk theology here. The attitude of "Anything you decide to believe is fine—do your own thing" is foreign to experiential theology. I'm asking for God's people to become more aware of the patterns in their faith pilgrimages. We must look for, listen to, and share what God is doing in us.

Theology always begins with God. And the God who is personal, relational, and redemptive is active in persons who are open and committed to him. We are experiencing God daily. As Billy Graham once said in response to the God-is-dead viewpoint, "God is alive. I know. I talked with him this morning." When we acknowledge the patterns of God's power in us, we become experiential theologians and can tell our own stories of infectious faith.

From Person to Congregation

When a group of Christians pool their experiences with God in a church community, a congregational body of belief emerges. Congregational theology is usually too hit-or-miss to be symmetrical. This congregational belief system isn't easily summed up. Churches try to express their doctrinal stances through covenants, confessions of faith, and even constitutions and bylaws. But these formal, written documents rarely reflect the real theology of a group.

How can you discover the belief system of your congregation? How do we move from personal stories to a congregation-wide belief system? James McClendon helps us move from the narrative theology of our own story to the controlling images of a convictional community, like the church. McClendon claims, "The best way to understand theology is to see it . . . as the investigation of the convictions of a convictional community."[2] What we believe, we do. Theology becomes visible when we act out our convictions in worship, discussion, and ministry. For example, the Lord's Supper celebration is pictured theology, an image regularly enacted to remind us of Christ's death for us. Baptism is another picture that becomes a demonstration of faith in a congregational setting. Jesus must have believed, "A picture is worth a thousand words." He gave us some visual celebrations to practice and vivid stories to repeat.

Congregational beliefs grow out of our history.[3] A congregation can explore some key shapers of its beliefs and practices by examining its corporate past.

ACTION EXERCISE #4

What Has Shaped Our Congregational Beliefs?

1. What are the special gifts of our congregation for which we're grateful?
2. What hurts or conflicts have we suffered and still resent?
3. Who have our key leaders and influencers been?
4. What have been the most important decisions we have made as a group during our history, and how do these decisions continue to shape us?

Singing Our Theology

I suspect the hymns a congregation sings regularly and with feeling are the best clue to the congregation's corporate theology. This is especially true when the congregation participates in choosing the hymns it sings. Congregational singing lends itself to the intuitive, spontaneous, repetitious, and corporate nature of experiential theology. For instance, the "concert" I overheard in the college dorm awakened me to the genius of music as an avenue for stating our theology. Likewise, most children who attend church regularly can sing choruses before they can recite Bible verses. Music shapes those who sing it.

Any doubter of the power of music has overlooked the omnipresent radio or tape player with teenage listeners singing the lyrics of currently popular songs. When these teens act out the philosophy the songs "sell," we can observe the mind-molding effect of music. Children's television shows, especially public broadcasting programs, make a more positive use of music to teach and entertain. Overall, however, the church may be losing the struggle to shape young lives through music to secular influences.

The person who chooses the hymns for worship is potentially the most important theologian in his congregation. His personal theology (or musical preference) will be a potent shaping force in the belief patterns of the church. Some ministers have a "don't repeat a hymn" rule and miss an excellent vehicle for undergirding the kingdom dream. Repeating hymns strategically can help a theological vision grow and help worship have more focus and impact. Trying to sing all the selections in the hymnal might make a congregation's theology broad but thin.

Recently a survey was done in 1,954 churches in 18 states.[4] The survey requested a list of the ten favorite hymns and songs in each congregation. The response was good: 1,381 or 71 percent. Such a phenomenally high return suggests the issue was seen as important to these churches.

"What a Friend We Have in Jesus" placed first in the total survey results. This old hymn is strongly Christ-centered. It speaks of a warm, personal relationship with the God who forgives and supports us. This hymn undoubtedly is a favorite because it awakens our vision of Christ and his kingdom in our midst.

Two Books, One Theme

The Bible and the hymnal are Christianity's two basic books. The Bible records God's revelation to man; the hymnal repeats man's response to God.[5] The Bible is full of songs featuring praise for Christ. The birth of Christ itself inspired several hymns of praise: the Annunciation by Gabriel (Luke 1:30-33), Mary's Magnificat (Luke 1:46-55), the angels' song called *Gloria in Excelsis* (Luke 2:14), and *Nunc Dimittis* by Simeon (Luke 2:29-32).

But hymns of praise aren't limited to the Gospels. The loftiest Christological statement in the New Testament, Philippians 2:5-11, appears to be a quotation from an existing Christian hymn. It's also interesting to note the first persecution of the church produced the first Christian hymn (Acts 4:24-30). Since the early church had no written record of Jesus' life and ministry, they told his story orally. Apparently, some believers set Jesus' words and works to music and sang "songs in the night," like Paul and Silas (Acts 16:25). These songs' consistent theme was praise of Christ.[6]

Like the Jews who sang the Old Testament psalms, we Christians sing our faith. If hymns provide a corporate expression of what your congregation believes, you can learn a great deal about your congregation's theology by building a profile of your group's favorite hymns. First, use worship bulletins to see what has been sung repeatedly over the past several years. Then, check to see if the hymns sung match the faith of the congregation by taking a favorite hymn survey of the entire congregation. Finally, consider this question, Does your congregation's praise extend its kingdom dream?

ACTION EXERCISE #5

Profiling the Doctrine We Sing

1. What hymns and songs are sung by our congregation? Repeatedly? With most enthusiasm?
2. What are the doctrinal themes and content of these best loved hymns and songs?
3. Who chooses the worship hymns and songs regularly? Does this hymn selection function offer the possibility of special influence in shaping the congregation's beliefs? When the congregation at-large chooses worship music are there apparent differences in the selections? Is the doctrinal content different when the congregation selects the worship music?
4. How do these favorite hymns and songs relate to, reflect on, or differ from the congregation's dream?

The kingdom dream of Jesus and the Bible's theme of Christological praise are linked in Christ himself. Christ inaugurated the kingdom of God; the kingdom is completed in Christ. "Jesus *is* the Kingdom," according to one theologian.[7] A congregation's kingdom dream and its praise of Christ can clarify and strengthen that theological and practical relationship.

Deepening Your Congregation's Beliefs

Using hymns and music that demonstrate and deepen your congregation's kingdom dream is a primary strategy in developing a healthy church. We in the church are typically and traditionally verbal in our preaching and teaching styles. Sermons and hymns are basic tools in helping theology become a natural part of the fabric of life.

Ministers can help expand the theological imaginations of their congregations by the way they preach and teach. For example, two ministers on a church staff used a dramatic dialogue approach for exploring the biblical incident of Paul and Silas' jailing (Acts 16). The sermon was the combined testimony of Paul and Silas on why they were willing to risk prison to be Christians. The hymn service began with the two ministers singing a duet and the congregation joining in on the "songs in the night." This style of preaching makes experiential theology a living reality. The congregation feels a heightened sense of involvement and participation. Another variation of this style is teaching the Bible by asking students to assume the roles of persons in the text. This approach allows participants to live Scripture from the "inside."

On one occasion I led a Youth group in a series of studies called "Now Sounds for New Christians." We selected several popular songs with strong messages, played and analyzed the themes of these songs, and then examined blocks of Scripture to see how the Bible dealt with these same issues. Most of the youngsters had never thought about what the music they listened to constantly was trying to sell them. Creating a conversation between contemporary music and mainstream concerns of the Bible helped them examine their values.

In a Lord's Supper service, an electric moment was created when during the retelling of the Last Supper story four worshipers suddenly stood, one after the other on a prearranged cue, and asked, "Lord, is it I?" (Matt. 26:20-25). The impact was so profound several worshipers reported they almost repeated the question aloud spontaneously. That's when experiential theology is really alive and well!

A congregation's belief system can also be strengthened by using visual means. The eye has been called the window of the soul. But the contemporary church has made sparing use of the visual dimension of theology.[8] Worship banners, Advent wreaths, festivals of the arts, and the single wedding candle all lend their visual impact to theological development.

A simple visual teaching aid pastors can use is a children's stewardship poster contest. Children express themselves forcefully through pictures because they have strong imaginations and don't have many words to work with yet. Children's art tends to go directly to the heart of an issue. Visual presentations can help a congregation make their kingdom dream more concrete and help them stay sharply focused on their dream.

Deciding on a local expression of the kingdom dream and taking congregational ownership of that dream is undergirded by a healthy belief system. Since worship is the most public occasion involving the largest number of the members, the musical and visual elements of worship need to be strategically selected. We can observe the patterns of our faith pilgrimages, tell our stories, and sing of the Christ who awakens our dream and defines our theology. The pastor is a powerful congregational theologian. He has a regular, public platform for articulating the kingdom dream.

Detour: A Fork in the Road

Let me detour a moment to signal a sharp psychological turn. Chapter 3 described the kingdom dream of a healthy church. This chapter has dealt with a healthy theological foundation to support the dream. Both are emotional and intuitive issues. Next we'll explore the goal system of a healthy church, a more rational concern. Before we move on to the subject of goals, let me note that we're making an important psychological transition in organizational studies. We're now moving from more intuitive to more rational organizational concerns.

Medical scientists have known for some time that different portions of the human brain controlled specific motor functions. For instance, it has long been recognized that the right side of the brain controlled the left side of the body and vice versa. Now, some exciting new research indicates a person tends to favor and use one side or hemisphere of his brain over the opposite side.[9] In other words, some of us are right-brained because we utilize primarily the right hemisphere of our brains; others of us are left-brained.

Let me compare and contrast the tendencies of each brain hemisphere:

Left Hemisphere	*Right Hemisphere*
More rational	More intuitive
Used more when awake	Used more while asleep
Deals well with facts	Handles emotions and feelings best
Linear operation with language and logic the most obvious faculties, verbal	Visual and operates holistically and relationally, processes several bits of information simultaneously, nonverbal
Uses Greek thought patterns	Uses Hebrew thought patterns
Occupationally, tends to be lawyers, accountants, and planners	Occupationally, tends to be artists, politicians, and managers
More closely related to Western psychology and the Adult ego state	More closely related to Eastern psychology and the Child ego state

From an organizational behavior perspective, we've been exploring dream and belief, two issues that relate more closely to the functioning of the right brain. Some persons will find themselves in tune with dream and belief more than goals and similar concerns. Their preference may well indicate the brain hemisphere they're most at home with. Picture the relationship of favored brain hemispheres to our health cycle model for organizations (p. 60).

Both brain hemispheres are needed for leading a congregation toward health. The diverse gifts in the body of Christ are especially crucial at this point (1 Cor. 12:14-26). The right hemisphere members of the congregation can lead where the strengths of vision, imagination, intuition, and feeling are needed. Where logic, plan-

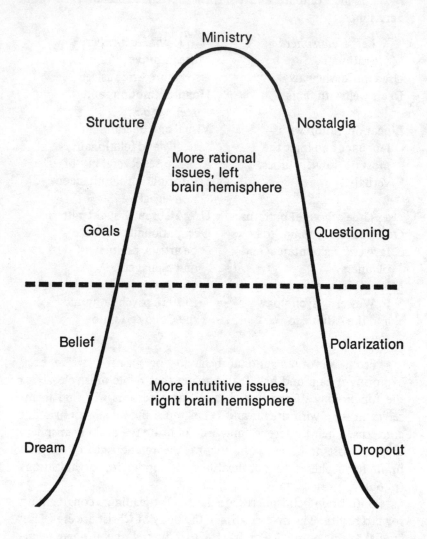

Ministry

Structure   Nostalgia

More rational
issues, left
brain hemisphere

Goals   Questioning

Belief   Polarization

More intuitive issues,
right brain hemisphere

Dream   Dropout

see p. 59

ning, and reasoning are demanded the left hemisphere church members can provide their gifts to organizational life. It's interesting to note that the Bible tends to be right-brained, but most theology is inclined to use the left hemisphere. American culture is also fairly heavily shaped by left-brain functioning. The church may need to learn how to use its right-brain hemisphere to dream and experience the theology it has developed with the left side. But balance in thought patterns is essential.[10] This may seem to be a revolutionary challenge, but it's necessary for church health and the use of spiritual gifts.

Notes

1. "That's Where I Learned to Sing My First Song," (North Carolina) *Biblical Recorder,* February 10, 1979, p. 2.

2. James William McClendon, Jr., *Biography as Theology: How Life Stories Can Remake Today's Theology* (Nashville: Abingdon Press, 1974), p. 35. McClendon suggests that we can understand a person's theology by understanding his biography. From outstanding Christians' writings, biographies, interview records, and reports from family and friends, McClendon extracts "controlling images or dominate motifs" of the persons he is studying. These images are acted out and form the "very substance of religion." See pages 87-111 for an explanation by McClendon of his method of doing experiential theology.

3. Sam Keen, *To a Dancing God* (New York: Harper & Row, Publishers, 1970), p. 73. Keen, in the context of a discussion on "storytelling and the discovery of identity," lists four questions he uses to help persons explore how they've come to be as they are. His questions are 1) what *wounds* or hurts do you resent having suffered?, 2) what *gifts* were you given for which you are grateful?, 3) who were your important *heroes* and models?, and 4) what were the crucial *decisions* for which you were responsible? I've restated these questions for a group or congregation to use in understanding what they believe and why they act as they do.

4. "Just a Minute," (Oklahoma) *Baptist Messenger,* September 15, 1977, p. 2.

5. Edmond D. Keith, *Christian Hymnody* (Nashville: Convention Press, 1956), p. 3.

6. Praise is typical of biblical songs, even in the Old Testament. The first biblical hymn, for example, is Moses' song of victory after the Red Sea deliverance (Ex. 15:1-18). Additionally, the Psalms are the faith of the Old Testament set to music. Most scholars think the hymn sung by Jesus and the apostles after the Last Supper was a Hallel Psalm (Pss. 113—118), a praise song (Matt. 26:30).

7. Harvey Cox, *The Secular City* (New York: The Macmillan Co., 1965), p. 111.

8. Lyle E. Schaller, *Hey, That's Our Church* (Nashville: Abingdon Press, 1975), pp. 141-143.

9. For a sampling of research on brain hemisphere functioning, see Howard Gardner, *The Shattered Mind* (New York: Alfred A. Knopf, 1975); Michael S. Gazzaniga, *The Bisected Brain* (New York: Appleton-Century Crofts, 1970); Robert E. Ornstein, "Right and Left Thinking," *Psychology Today*, Vol. 6 (1973), No. 12, pp. 87-93; Thomas S. Isaak, "What Trainers Need to Know About Both Halves of the Brain," *Training HRD*, January, 1978, pp. 27-30; George Prince, "Putting the Other Half of the Brain to Work," *Training HRD*, November, 1978, pp. 57-61; and Henry Mintzberg, "Planning on the Left Side and Managing on the Right," *Harvard Business Review*, July-August, 1976, pp. 49-58.

10. James B. Ashbrook and Paul W. Walaskay, *Christianity for Pious Skeptics* (Nashville: Abingdon Press, 1977), pp. 89-160.

5

Turning Dreams into Deeds

"Man's mind, stretched by a new idea, never goes back to its original dimensions," claimed Oliver Wendell Holmes. The same is true for healthy congregations. Once a church has been grasped by its kingdom dream and strengthens its belief system it cannot turn back from its mission. In the words of a friend, "Once you've seen Jerusalem, you'll always be a wandering Jew!" A vision changes life. Dream and belief become the fertile seedbeds for congregational goals.

"Now faith is the turning of dreams into deeds" is Clarence Jordan's paraphrase of Hebrews 11:1.[1] That's a good definition of congregational goals too. Turning kingdom dreams into deeds of ministry is a prime goal for every church. The dream puts a positive flavor to church goals. Some congregations use the *needs + resources = goals* equation for goal setting. Too often they define needs as problems and resources are viewed mostly as limiting factors. Their goals have a defeatist flavor in advance.

A better goal setting formula is: *needs + resources x kingdom dream = church goals.* The kingdom dream challenges negative thinking and puts a theological foundation under our dreams-into-deeds goals.

Mission or Survival?

Church goals generally fall into two categories: mission and survival.[2] Either a congregation joins God in redemptive "co-mis-

63

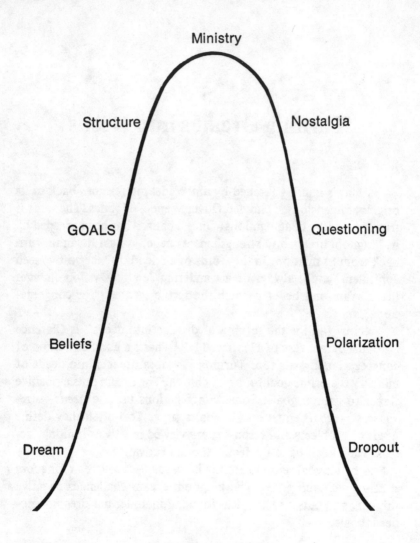

Ministry

Structure   Nostalgia

GOALS   Questioning

Beliefs   Polarization

Dream   Dropout

sion" or it tries simply to hang on, keeps the doors open, lights on, and the organizational machinery turning. A church plans for health and growth or settles for surviving and solving problems. Donald Metz's research found that churches, which had either lost touch with their kingdom dream, or, worse yet, had never had a clearly stated purpose at all, characteristically took one of two actions to survive: 1) conflicted with and/or fired their minister as a vent for their frustrations, or, 2) built a building and plunged themselves into the clearer goal of paying a monthly mortgage debt.

Most new congregations have three survival tasks. The survival goals are the actions necessary to continue institutional life: gathering a congregation, erecting a building, and solidifying a budget. Many established churches find survival goals can become ends in themselves. The declining church may drift into a problem-solving stance and find itself constantly fighting brush fires and giving little or no thought to planning and going on mission.

Another challenge occurs when a settled congregation discovers the hidden agenda of its founding dream was survival. The early enthusiasm characteristic of a new congregation may have centered on the unity of survival tasks.

Try to visualize mission goals on the up side of the health cycle and survival goals on the down side. Mission builds off of planning; survival is a problem-solving process.

Where Do Goals Come From?

A congregation's goals have a variety of sources and may be formal or informal. Formal goals are those actions the congregation explores and openly commits itself to do. Informal goals are what the members want to see happen in the congregation, but for a variety of reasons these actions aren't adopted by the group as a whole. Whether formal or informal, a congregation's goals are likely to divide themselves watershed fashion into two categories of goals: issues of mission and ministry or issues of survival and maintenance.

Several key forces help shape goals. *Goal shapers* are the spin-offs of dream and belief that provide the emotional energy for congregational goal setting. Three goal shapers are especially significant. The *minister's outlook* is a basic source of church goals. "Each leader . . . has a vision and strives to make reality conform with it. Some visions call for a complete transformation; others entail marginal change."[3] The minister's dream spills over and mixes with the hopes of key leaders to become goals.

Another goal-shaping factor is the *climate* of the congregation. An atmosphere settles over a church that tempers its outlook and, therefore, its goals. Some congregations are warm, optimistic, and aggressive in their viewpoint. Others are apathetic and inert, showing few signs of life. Still other churches are negative and defensive. The climate determines the morale level and congregational sense of direction to a large extent.

③ *Stakeholders' expectations* are the most significant goal shapers. Not all members of a church feel they have a stake in the organizational life of the congregation. But some participants move from casual curiosity to deep commitment. They develop and express a sense of psychological ownership.[4] Stakeholders make an emotional investment of vision, energy, time, and money in their congregation. This psychological phenomenon parallels the stockholder who buys into a publicly-owned company.

Stakeholding goes deeper than a mere sense of belonging to a group. For stakeholders, the group's life belongs to them. Emotional ownership is especially apparent in congregational goals. Lyle Schaller defines a good goal as "one that I have had a part in formulating. A bad goal is one that someone else developed and wants me to implement."[5] Stakeholders feel a personal involvement in, responsibility for, and loyalty to their church that goes beyond assigned or delegated tasks. A decline in participation or financial support, low morale, staffing difficulties, communication gaps, and poor planning are marks of a lack of stakeholding in a church or volunteer organization.

Goal strategies [6] grow out of the decisions of the goal shapers.

These strategies range from extremely positive to completely negative. The most radical goal type is the *new-growth* strategy. This approach tries to diversify into totally new ministry areas and is willing to take risks in order to grow. A slightly less progressive strategy is *extension growth* which extends growth selectively by spinning off ministries from an already established base. The most common middle-of-the-road goal type is to *preserve.* A preservation goal is one which holds its ground and defends the ministries of the past. A conservative strategy is to *phase out* ministries which have passed their peak. The goal strategy that is viewed as most negative or remedial is to *exit* or quit a ministry now. For a model of a church goal system see page 68.

Goals by Default

Organizations can soon develop a life and momentum of their own. They may drift along down the path of least resistance. The goals of the church during times of drift are generally goals by default. No one chooses or decides or directs, so the organization uses its members' time, energy, money, and church properties without a sense of mission.

Default goals come in several varieties. *Repeating last year* is a default goal. Planning becomes a habitual matter of doing again what has been done before. Leaders try to maintain business as usual and keep routines from becoming too deadening. One minister who had served the same congregation for a decade summed up defaulting to last year graphically, "After having walked around this barn for ten years, you learn where to step! The calendar looks the same every year." Ministry by repetition is ordinarily out of touch with the kingdom dream.

The *real estate agenda* can become a default goal too.[7] Debt is a clear-cut survival goal because there are legal and moral obligations to pay loans on buildings and properties. But an "edifice complex" may contribute marginally to a kingdom dream. One well-to-do young church made a crucial mission-or-survival decision. It had established itself successfully and had paid off its initial

CHURCH GOALS

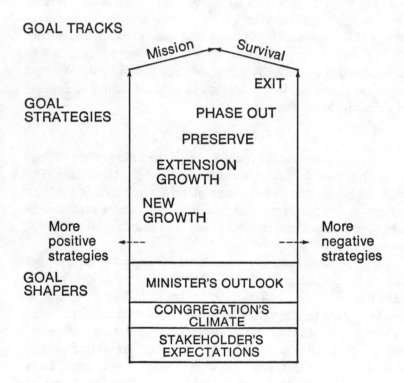

GOAL TRACKS

Mission ← → Survival

GOAL
STRATEGIES

EXIT

PHASE OUT

PRESERVE

EXTENSION
GROWTH

NEW
GROWTH

More
positive
strategies ← - - - - - → More
negative
strategies

GOAL
SHAPERS

MINISTER'S OUTLOOK

CONGREGATION'S
CLIMATE

STAKEHOLDER'S
EXPECTATIONS

building and property mortgages. With almost unlimited resources of people, finances, and talent, it could go on mission. Instead, it built a $750,000 wedding chapel. Even though many members were influential citizens, they couldn't fill the large sanctuary for a wedding. A smaller replica of the sanctuary was constructed on an adjacent lot and has been used exclusively for weddings. Plunging into debt makes real estate the survival agenda and may limit ministry possibilities.

③ Busywork can be goal setting by default also. Busywork is created work or things people do to pass time. Detail work done on goals contributing to the kingdom dream isn't considered busyness for activity's sake.

One expression of busywork occurs when individual satisfaction displaces group goals.[8] When persons in an organization pursue their own goals and allow group goals to lag, the group may settle for busyness. Some tension between individual and group goals is always present in organizations, but the energy focus of healthy congregations remains on the dream of the total membership.

Indicators of Church Goals

Your church budget and calendar are the primary documents of the living history of your congregation. The budget and calendar also reveal your church's operating priorities and often develop a pattern of their own. One pastor bemoaned the overcrowded calendar of his church. He feared, with tongue in cheek, that his congregation would have to cancel Christmas and Easter for lack of calendar time! He had found too many "traditional activities" threatened to crowd out really festive days.

Budgets also tend to get rutted so that old organizations and traditional projects get funded year after year—even if they no longer make an important contribution to the kingdom dream. In a former church of mine, the congregation chose to devote six months to intensive evangelism and outreach work. We agreed that funds and calendar time for all program organizations would be measured by their contribution to the evangelistic goal. The most difficult issue in structuring and programming toward this goal was the persistent "we've *always* done (or spent) it this way before" chorus. Even though the goal was clearly defined and freely and overwhelmingly chosen, we discovered that personal and organizational ruts were deeply worn and threatened our vision.

Does your church budget reflect and develop your church's dream? You may discover your church budget has lost its direct relation to the dream. Organizations and programs no longer supporting the primary mission of your church may be receiving disproportionate amounts of the budget and calendar time.

ACTION EXERCISE #6

Values Shown by Our Budget

1. How does our church actually spend its budget?
    Mostly on buildings and properties?
    Mostly on personnel salaries?
    Mostly on national and foreign missions?
    Mostly on local ministry and outreach?
    Mostly on church education programs?
2. Do our budget expenditures flow outward on mission or inward on maintaining our congregation?
3. Which age groups are spotlighted via budgeted funds?
4. Which organizations get the most money?
5. Do we have any organizations or groups which have no access to budgeted funds?

Goals and budget are closely intertwined. But goals precede budgets. Goals are set first, then budgets are developed. Otherwise the budget becomes the accidental goal system of the church. Either we fund our dream or we probably just dream of funds.

What Makes a Goal Real?

Why are some church goals formally adopted but never implemented? They aren't real goals. Unmet goals are usually the result of a low commitment by stakeholders. But real goals—ones that are valued by stakeholders whether they are formal or informal goals—are almost always achieved. People do what they feel strongly about.

The real goals of a church are its organizational values. We act on our values.[9] They become the motivational catapults for what we achieve individually and congregationally. As a dream is internalized and concretized by an individual, it becomes a personal value. As the congregation begins to take ownership of the dream's values corporately, they become the group's goals. Group values set the direction for organizations.

Christian organizations are distinctive in part because they have an allegiance higher even than their organizational goals. Christian groups have an eternal, redemptive value system. They have a dream, and their vision transcends their short-term goals.[10]

Leaders who want to create and implement real goals will involve as many people as practical in goal setting. People support what they help create. When the formally adopted goals of a group match the individual values of group members, real goals are evident and become virtually irresistible.

Supporting Mission Goals

When a congregation chooses to go on mission rather than settling for survival, two supportive strategies can be implemented. First, leaders can build on the energy reservoirs of the congregation. Certain persons have energy for some projects or issues. Their enthusiasm and excitement for their pet projects may be almost fanatical. Sometimes persons or groups in a congregation discover mutual interests, form a coalition, and pool their energies. These merged energies form reservoirs that become significant resources for organizational life when they are recognized and channeled.

Energy reservoirs are evidence of motivation; this scarce commodity must be used for kingdom dream ministry.

ACTION EXERCISE #7

Looking for Energy Reservoirs

1. What do people volunteer for in our church?
2. What do our members show enthusiasm for, get excited about, and have a willingness to do?
3. What does our church budget time and money for gladly?

Secondly, leaders must provide adequate recognition channels. Volunteers are paid in satisfaction, growth, service, and recognition. Lyle Schaller notes some congregations award their members high honors—like the Boy Scouts of America's Silver Beaver award. Other congregations, by contrast, hand out "dead rats."[11] Without adequate recognition, even highly motivated volunteers lose their enthusiasm for work. Stroke deprivation, or a lack of recognition, lowers individual morale.

ACTION EXERCISE #8

Evaluating Our Recognition Pattern

1. What are people honored for in our church?
2. What does it take to get a thank you, a public recognition, a certificate of appreciation, a memorial plaque, your name listed in the worship bulletin or church newsletter, or a personal letter from the minister?
3. Who is honored?
4. How are they honored? By whom? When?
5. Are some church posts partly or totally honorary? How are these honorary offices assigned?

Linking Goals with Dream

Goals should grow directly out of dream and belief. People respond well to specific, tangible goals. Many tangible goals, like building programs, Youth choir trips, property renovation, emergency needs, and mission tours tend to be survival oriented.

How can we develop tangible mission goals? Two applications of linking goals with the dream need to be made.

● Make projects and goals that implement the church's dream very "sense-able." Try to make the goals so real and concrete that they can almost be seen, touched, and tasted. The kingdom dream can transform some normally survival-oriented goals into mission and ministry goals.

● Make sure building programs are dream resources. Tie them directly to the mission of the congregation by planning people-oriented ministry in your buildings. Use the buildings flexibly.

Building programs are crucial congregational actions. They (1) drain off enormous amounts of members' energies and (2) may subtly shift the goal focus of the congregation from "let's go on mission and reach people" to "let's stay on mission enough to pay our debts." Professional planning assistance may be helpful in discovering the long-range needs of your community and congregation.

Link your congregation's goals to its dream. That's the surest way to turn kingdom dreams into deeds of ministry.

Comissioned to Develop Dream Goals

Christians share in God's redemptive mission. We are on "co-mission" with him in turning dreams into deeds. Congregational leaders are always challenged to focus resources on redemptive goals. Several strategies assist the development of dream goals:[12]

● Keep the dream public. Preach it. Teach it. Orient new members to it. Give members many opportunities to talk about God's work in our world. Help them experience redemption as "co-mission."

● Formalize goals. Arrange for forums where aspects of the dream can be examined, debated, clarified, and committed to. New ideas from members will enrich and excite. Special interest groups may be confronted. The intent is to adopt formally the dream of the stakeholders.

● Establish priorities. No church can accomplish its kingdom dream entirely through one budget or calendar or program. Congregations are rarely that rich in resources. Slice off the most crucial aspect of the dream that's attainable now and go to work.

● State your goals specifically. Goals are generalizations by nature. Translate your goals into concrete, limited, realistic, and important statements of action. Ministry projects lend themselves to finely honed goals. Remember a workable goal is specific, attainable, and measurable.

● Distribute responsibility. Stakeholder goals attract workers by definition. People support what they create and value. Broaden the base of participation so all may be involved in turning dreams into tangible deeds.

● Evaluate at regular intervals. When progress is made toward goals, celebrate. When a congregation gets off target, make a mid-course correction. Evaluation is essential as a congregational guidance system.

Turning dreams into deeds is the process of incarnation. Just as God in Christ became flesh (John 1:14), contemporary Christians embody the dream and turn it into incarnated deeds of ministry and mission.

Notes

1. Clarence L. Jordan, *Cotton Patch Version of Hebrews and the General Epistles* (New York: Association Press, 1973).
2. Donald L. Metz, *New Congregations* (Philadelphia: Westminster Press, 1967). In fairness it should be noted that Metz studied a small group

of new Presbyterian congregations on the West Coast. His findings, however, seem to have fairly wide application to churches in general.

3. William E. Rothschild, *Putting It All Together: A Guide to Strategic Thinking* (New York: AMACOM, 1976), p. 15.

4. Richard Beckhard, *Organization Development: Strategies and Models* (Reading, Massachusetts: Addison-Wesley Publishing Co., Inc., 1969), p. 19; Rothschild, p. 20.

5. Lyle E. Schaller, *Survival Tactics in the Parish* (Nashville: Abingdon Press, 1977), p. 161.

6. Rothschild, pp. 15-21.

7. Schaller, p. 107.

8. Arthur M. Adams, *Effective Leadership for Today's Church* (Philadelphia: Westminster Press, 1978), pp. 79-80.

9. For an explanation of values, see Louis Raths, Merrill Harmin, and Sidney B. Simon, *Values and Teaching* (Columbus, Ohio: Charles E. Merrill, 1966) and Brian Hall, *Value Clarification as a Learning Process* (New York: Paulist/Newman Press, 1972. For a view of values in institutional life, see Maury Smith, "Some Implications of Value Clarification for Organizational Development," *The 1973 Annual Handbook for Group Facilitators* (San Diego, California: University Associates, 1973), pp. 203-211.

10. Ted W. Engstrom and Edward R. Dayton, *The Art of Management for Christian Leaders* (Waco, Texas: Word, Inc., 1976), pp. 15-16.

11. Schaller, pp. 80-90.

12. Donald L. Metz, "The Task of Translation," *Your Church*, May/June, 1979, pp. 30,39.

6
Structure: Muscle for Ministry

Everything needs some structure to work well. For example, people have a structural picture in their heads of how the world works. Once after delivering a lecture on the solar system, William James was confronted by a little, old lady. She took exception to his explanation of the earth as a ball rotating around the sun.

Rather, she proposed to James, "We live on a crust of earth on the back of a giant turtle."

In an effort to avoid abrasiveness, William James asked, "Madam, what does the turtle stand on?"

"You're very clever," replied the little lady, "but I can answer your question. The first turtle stands on the back of a second, far larger turtle."

"But what does the second turtle stand on?" persisted James.

Triumphantly, the little lady announced, "It's no use, Mr. James. It's turtles all the way down!"

Organization gives the dream something to stand on and to work through. Organization lends muscular structure to churches. Structure is essential for form, strength, and purposeful life. Formal organization exists to do work, to pursue ministry goals. Informal organization emerges to meet needs. Whether formal or informal, structure helps congregations do their work "decently and in order" (1 Cor. 14:40).

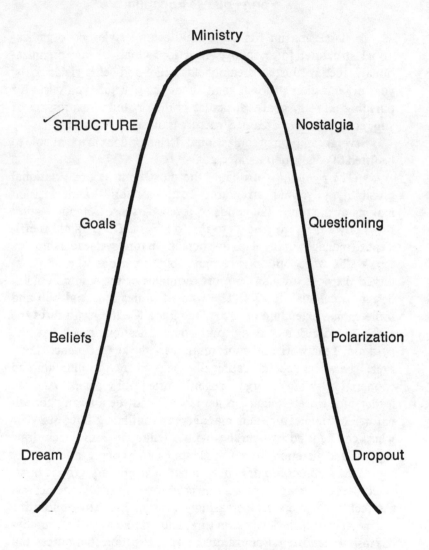

Form Follows Function

A classic maxim fits both architectural style and organizational structure: (form follows function) Goals dictate organizational structure. Just as dream yields belief and belief yields goals, your organization's formal goals shape the structure you select for pursuing ministry goals. Structure is the organized expression of your congregation's dream. Structure is muscle for ministry.

Several common organizational design options are available to be fitted to your group's stated goals.[1]

/-• The *pyramid* is probably the most familiar organizational possibility. Pyramid structures focus authority and decision making at the top in the hands of a few persons. Communication flows down from the leaders to the followers. The pyramid is efficient to manage but involves few persons in top-level leadership.

2-• The *wheel* option is recognizable to persons who have observed the pods on many airport terminals or the commonwealth design in colonial politics. The wheel features a central hub and some spokes extending out from the hub. The hub centralizes the authority, decision making, and communication, much like the pyramid. Teamwork and coordination are the key differences however. The wheel depicts graphically the need for coordination and cooperation within an organization's varied work groups. And the leader of a wheel-designed organization must be a strong coordinator, communicator, and manager of conflicting interests. The wheel can be used by churches with satellite missions which draw support and direction from a single sponsoring congregation.

5-• *Task forces* are design options for temporary groups organized to solve a single problem or produce one item. Some observers feel our society is increasingly gearing itself to nonroutine organizations, throwaway structures and "ad-hocracy."[2] Churches use task forces often. For example, pastor selection committees and many long-range planning groups use a task-force structure. When their specific, assigned task is completed, they dissolve and cease to function.

 ✓• _Matrix_ structures are also becoming popular organizational design possibilities.³ In fact, project management is becoming a new management science in itself. An outgrowth of the space program during the 1960s, matrix organizations are designed to coordinate two functions—like research and production—at once. The matrix approach requires enough specialized training and full-time coordination that many volunteer organizations find it too demanding to manage comfortably.

United We Stand

All organizations are social systems regardless of the structural option(s) they choose to pursue their goal(s). Let me define and illustrate some technical systems terms briefly. Social systems are patterns of relationships (1) with a number of parts or subsystems; (2) with connections, or interfaces, allowing interdependence with communication among the parts; (3) with the whole greater than the simple sum of the parts, or synergy; and (4) with adjustments necessary throughout the system when any subsystem changes or the ripple effect.

Think of your church as a social system. Churches have long sensed the organic nature of "the body of Christ" (Rom. 12:4-8; 1 Cor. 12:12-31). In a congregation, the subsystems are the classes, fellowship groups, and committees. Church interfaces are the councils and coordination settings in which the different subsystems meet and work. Synergy occurs when the dream goals are owned and implemented by all or most of the membership so that momentum occurs and morale lifts. The ripple effect reminds church leaders of a systems' rule: you can't change just one thing. Any change jars the entire system and sets off a struggle for a new equilibrium.

A friend's experience with a new car illustrates how systems work. He bought a brand-new auto and drove it proudly. One Saturday morning, however, he couldn't get the transmission to go into gear. The shift lever moved freely but wasn't meshing with the transmission. The car wouldn't budge. A quick examination by a

good
e.g.•

mechanically-minded neighbor revealed a missing cotter pin in the shift lever, a tiny but crucial item. My friend complained to his wife about how shoddily cars are made these days and how all the enjoyment of having a new car was now tainted. She listened patiently to his description of a cotter pin, slipped a bobby pin out of her hair, and handed the pin to him. In a few minutes a bobby pin had become a temporary cotter pin, and the car was functioning like new again. One small element had stopped a large machine completely. A cotter pin seemed insignificant by itself but happened in this case to be a vital part of the system.

Form follows function. The ministry you want to provide or the goal you want to attain determines the structure you use. Formal organization is important because it either helps you reach your ministry goals or creates a barrier which frustrates ministry and dulls the dream.

The Church Within the Church

Martin Luther described the existence of *ecclesiola* within the *ecclesia*—a church within the church. An organizational expression of this phenomenon is the informal organizational structure which develops within the formal structure of a church.

Informal structure emerges spontaneously from the natural attempts of members to meet their mutual needs.[4] Remember, in contrast, formal structure exists to pursue organizational goals. In reality, the formal and informal structures move a congregation along on two, sometimes conflicting, tracks. Conflict occurs when informal needs don't match formal objectives. For example, the social ties and kinship loyalties, communication patterns, and organizational habits may be more influential than the stated goals of a congregation. A church may vote to do a ministry and then ignore the implementation of the ministry because it doesn't meet their personal needs after all.

✗ Informal organization serves several functional needs.

1 — • The need to *belong.* People need to be included in groups offering close relationships. Each of us needs an occasional

shoulder to cry on, a sympathetic ear for emotional support and personal problem solving. Formal organizations are ordinarily task oriented and make relational issues secondary. But when we need encouragers, sounding boards, and confidants, informal friendship networks naturally emerge to meet our need to belong. Formal goals rarely deal with our belonging needs adequately.

2—• The need to know. People in organizations need to be "in the know" and feel like insiders. Most organizations have formal channels for sharing information—newsletters, posters, announcement periods, bulletin boards, and memos. But some issues which organizational participants are curious about aren't official business items. Therefore, every organization develops a "grapevine."

Grapevines are intriguing and useful organizational phenomena. (1) Information can begin anywhere in an organization. For instance, a new president of a denominational agency quickly found his best source of system-wide information was the institution's inside mailman. The mailman visited every work unit daily and enjoyed such a wide range of relationships that he knew virtually everybody and everything. The president learned to listen to the mailman and to cultivate the grapevine by telling the mailman selected tidbits to be shared on his rounds. (2) Information spreads rapidly in all directions like ripples on a pond. (3) Three of every four pieces of grapevine information are generally accurate. However, inaccurate items usually are greatly distorted and can become examples of rumor mongering. Even rumors contain emotional messages which may be accurate. That is, rumors' content may be untrue, but their feeling tone may be on target.

(4) Grapevine information can be coded. Jargon or in-jokes can reveal meanings to insiders while outsiders are left uninformed or confused. The book of Revelation is a biblical example of this phenomenon. (5) Grapevine information can be shared selectively. People can be deliberately bypassed and excluded from informal information networks. (6) Sometimes proximity affects the flow of grapevine information. While leading a staff retreat, I noticed the Youth minister was often addressed with "John, I don't know you,

but . . ." After probing why John wasn't known to his staff peers after three years of working with them, I discovered John's office was in the gym rather than in the church office area. The other staffers didn't know John because he was physically removed from them and was part of a different grapevine within a very large congregation.

I learned about community grapevines during my first pastorate. When I would return to the church field from school, I discovered the fastest way to catch up on community information was to call the telephone operator. The rural area around my church was served by a central telephone switchboard with all calls placed by an operator who evidently didn't hesitate to listen in. One call to her and the question, "Sarah, do you know of folks I need to see?" gave me information on the sick and troubled persons I needed to visit.

In a later pastorate, I found a network of women in the church spent long hours talking to each other on the phone daily. Whenever some kinds of information needed to be circulated over the church grapevine, I'd call the "telephone ladies." An announcement like "I know you'll be saddened to hear Mrs. Jones has just died; as you talk to people today, let them know about the funeral arrangements," never failed to get the word around the membership via the informal grapevine.

3. • The need to _understand expectations._ Members need to be aware of the "rules" of their organization. The expectations and values of a group govern its behavior and attitudes. In some informal structures, for example, the expectations get translated into powerful mottoes, such as, "You scratch my back and I'll scratch your back" or "Everyone pulls his weight" or "No one works too hard or looks too good." These expectation statements are rarely formal policy, but members soon learn they are the unspoken rules of their organization.

4. • The need to _be protected._ People know instinctively there's safety in numbers. So we band together to keep from being oppressed. Collectively people have power and courage to attempt

things they wouldn't try individually. Lobbies, strikes, boycotts, unions, and pressure groups are prime examples of the tendency toward protection through group organization.

Every church develops a power structure, a pecking order of authority. If the formal power structure and decision-making channels of a congregation become too closed, an informal "underground" emerges to equalize or veto the power of the regular channels. When informal authority patterns run counter to the formal ones, it's usually impossible for formal authority to control completely the informal need for protection. In other words, closed power structures invite an underground to form for the protection of the less powerful members of the organization.

Ministry Through Your Church's Informal Organization

Informal structure offers an untapped resource for ministers. Why? Because informal organization fills gaps in meeting needs, an area in which formal organizations tend to be negligent by their nature. A needs-meeting congregation uses both its informal and formal structures well. The capacity to use both formal and informal structures is one mark of a healthy church.

Ministers can remind themselves of three occasions when informal structure becomes crucial.

• When personal needs are unmet. Formal structure is geared to goals more than needs. Rather than being threatened when the natural needs for belonging, knowing, understanding expectations, and being protected surface, look for ways to minister through the informal structures that develop automatically. Since informal structures meet needs, ask yourself these questions. What need isn't being met through formal organizational channels? Is the unmet need legitimate? Could the need be met through formal structures? If not, am I willing deliberately to use informal organizational channels to meet real needs?

• When members are unsure leaders care for them. When the leaders of a congregation's formal structures listen to and show genuine concern for members, the informal structure becomes somewhat less important. The Golden Rule is applicable in organizational settings too.

3 • When members aren't involved in goal setting. When church members know, understand, and have participated in shaping the formal goals of their congregation, the informal organization becomes less crucial. The deeper and broader the ownership of organizational goals, the more likely members are to trust the leaders and the formal structures.

If persons feel like outsiders to formal structures, they'll build an informal system in which they can feel like insiders, a clique if necessary. Wise ministers open up the formal processes of decision making and goal setting to all of their congregation. Then they use informal structures to minister humanely to persons who still feel excluded at some point.

For the minister, formal structure is a church management challenge. That is, resources must be focused on ministry goals. Management lends direction and order. But informal structure is a leadership challenge. The minister must be a humane pacesetter, one who meets needs in Christ's name. Leadership takes initiative and models ministry. The creative minister both manages formal goals and leads in meeting personal needs.[5] He helps his church develop goals that focus ministry beyond the congregation generally, and uses informal networks to minister to members.

ACTION EXERCISE #9

Clues to Informal Structure

1. If you wanted to test a ministry idea with someone in your congregation, with whom would you talk? Who is the key "legitimizer," the person who justifies ideas as correct, reasonable, and fitting, in your congregation?

   Who is your church's "quarterback," the person

whose power can reverse a developing decision or whose opinion can declare a ministry option out-of-bounds?

2. When you have a personal burden, with whom do you talk about it in your church?
   When members want the advice of another layperson, with whom do they talk in your congregation?

3. If you had just returned from vacation and wanted to know what the church and community need situation is, whom would you ask?
   If you wanted to circulate ministry information, with whom would you share the information, and, thereby, cultivate the grapevine?

Structure and Systems: The Ministry of Organization

How much structure is enough for organizations? Enough to carry out dream goals. Any under-organized congregation has aspects of its dream unrepresented by a focused organizational unit. An over-organized congregation either has organizational units which aren't vital to its dream or has units representing goals already met.[6] While formal goals are rarely attained without organization, many organizational units outlive or outgrow their usefulness and call for pruning. Structure requires ongoing evaluation in order to keep it finely tuned for implementing dream goals.[7] Well-managed structure is necessary for a healthy congregation.

The minister serves a generalist role within a congregation. From an organizational viewpoint, he is charged with seeing the big picture of the dream goals, with maintaining a corporate perspective. Two types of personalities challenge the minister's system-wide wiew. The layperson with a specialist's perspective, a person who is a one-issue or one-organizational unit loyalist, is a challenge. Stretching this member's horizons may allow him to take ownership of most or all of the congregation's dream. Occasionally, the minister encounters a layperson who also possesses a corporate vision, a generalist's view, too. If the minister's threat level can be curbed, the generalist layperson can become a valuable ally and sounding board.

Ministry through structure and throughout systems is an exciting possibility for the minister who accepts his stewardship of organizational resources. Structure and systems provide the muscle and sinew for attaining congregational goals.

Notes

1. O. Jeff Harris, Jr., *Managing People at Work* (New York: John Wiley & Sons, Inc., 1976), pp. 79-108; Ross A. Webber, "Staying Organized," *Wharton Magazine*, Spring, 1979, pp. 16-23; Louis A. Allen, *Management and Organization* (New York: McGraw-Hill Book Co., 1958), pp. 51-71; Ernest Dale, *Organization* (New York: AMACOM, 1967), pp. 27-48; Joseph A. Letterer, *The Analysis of Organization* (New York: John Wiley & Sons, 1967), pp. 397-414; and Bertram M. Gross, *Organizations and Their Managing* (New York: Free Press, 1964), pp. 197-237.

2. Alvin Toffler, *Future Shock* (New York: Random House, Inc., 1970), p. 121.

3. Stanley M. Davis and Paul R. Lawrence, *Matrix* (Reading, Massachusetts: Addison-Wesley Publishing Co., Inc., 1977); and Norman Wright, "Matrix Management: A Primer for the Administrative Manager," *Management Review*, April, 1979, pp. 58-61, May, 1979, pp. 59-62, and June, 1979, pp. 57-58.

4. O. Jeff Harris, Jr., *Managing People at Work* (New York: John Wiley & Sons, 1976), pp. 111-132; Keith Davis, "Togetherness: the Informal Variety" in Donald M. Bowman and Francis M. Fillerup, *Management: Organization and Planning* (New York: McGraw-Hill Book Co., 1963), pp. 41-52; and Bertram M. Gross, *Organizations and Their Managing* (New York: Free Press, 1964), pp. 238-259.

5. Robert K. Greenleaf, *Servant Leadership* (New York: Paulist/Newman Press, 1977), pp. 59-60.

6. Arthur Merrihew Adams, *Effective Leadership for Today's Church* (Philadelphia: Westminster Press, 1978), p. 89.

7. George S. Odiorne, "Clearing Corporate Deadwood: the Practical

Art of Pruning Organizational Limbs," *Management Review*, June, 1979, pp. 39-44; Ernest Dale, *Organization* (New York: AMACOM, 1967), pp. 189-202; and Louis A. Allen, *Management and Organization* (New York: McGraw-Hill Book Co., 1958), pp. 273-307.

7

The Promise and Threat of Ministry

Ministry, from an organizational perspective, is the kingdom dream incarnated. Christian ministry is a vision come to life in cups of cold water, visits to hospitals and prisons, and meals for the hungry (Matt. 25:34-40). Ministry is words of witness to non-Christians. It is encouragement for the homeless, orphans, singles, aged, and formerly marrieds. Ministry supports persons with fragmented emotions and fractured relationships. In short, ministry helps persons in Christ's name. The kinds of ministry actions are limited only by our vision and others' needs.

The length of a congregation's ministry is virtually endless. But when ministry loses its focus on extending and expanding God's kingdom, an organizational plateau occurs. Organizational senility sets in. Ministry begins to slip. The organizational aging process is often nudged along by, paradoxically, the congregation's strong commitment to practical ministries. Lyle Schaller notes that "any move in the direction of becoming more sensitive to the needs of people increases the complexity of the operation."[1] A congregation must stay in touch with its dream, on the one hand, and its unique opportunities for ministry, on the other hand. Otherwise it may inadvertently shorten the duration of its effective ministry.

Other factors impede dream-based ministry too. Time passes and people forget basic purposes and beginnings. New ministers and members bring in varied backgrounds and interests. Congrega-

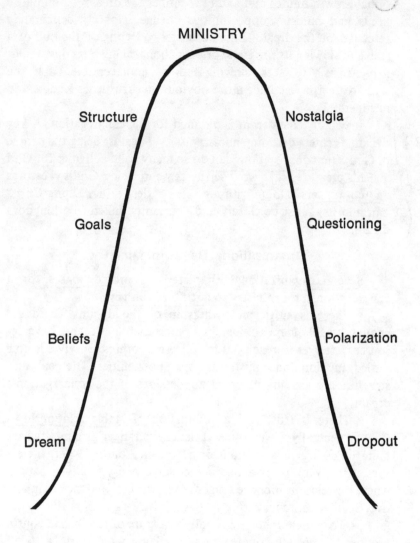

MINISTRY

Structure   Nostalgia

Goals   Questioning

Beliefs   Polarization

Dream   Dropout

tional growth dilutes and subtly redefines the dream. Community needs and ministry opportunities change. Nobody deliberately refocuses on the dream. Like barnacles collecting on the hull of a ship and slowing its progress, organizational aging bogs down ministry efforts. At first the slowing is almost imperceptible. Later, the sense of inertia becomes more obvious and frustrates leaders and members alike.

Inevitably, the dream is dimmed for the congregation. A key dynamic centers on doing ministry as over against being the people of God. Our congregations can do so many good activities for God and his creatures that we lose the sense of being God's creatures and "co-workers." Doing without being is deadening. Doing Christian ministry must be closely and constantly linked to a kingdom dream.

Organizational Bases for Ministry

Several organizational characteristics provide bases for a congregation at the ministry stage of the health cycle.

1. • There is sufficient ownership of the dream. There are enough stakeholders to sustain organizational life and have resources left over to reach out in concern to others. Survival is now settled; mission and ministry are open possibilities. The goals and structure are yielding practical applications of the congregation's dream.

2. • There is trust and a foundation of stable relationships. Groups generally are of three varieties: "stranger groups," where there are no previous relationships; "cousin groups," where there's some history of prior acquaintanceships; and "family groups," where the relationships are longer term, warmer, and more supportive. Smaller churches with effective ministries are primarily family groups. Larger churches are usually a mixture of family and cousin groups. Ministering congregations display a team spirit, a "we" climate. Members know each other and work together in an extended family atmosphere.

3 • The needs of persons are being met. The formal goals and structure are focused on concern for persons external to the church. And the informal organization is ministering to the needs of members. In the words of Sam Keen concerning structured ministry, "Caring must be made concrete, otherwise there is no incarnation, no fleshing-out of love. . . . Organization is the embodiment of love."[2]

4 • Volunteers are adequately paid in recognition, growth, and challenge. They feel blessed and are willing to become blessings to others.

5 • The morale level of the members is high. The energy reservoirs of motivation are numerous and full.

6 • The norms of the organization are healthy and growth enhancing.

Norms: Watershed of Organizational Health

Norms are the habits of an organization.[3] Norms are the unconsidered "standard operating procedures" of a group or institution. The unspoken rules, routines, patterns, and traditions of an organization give it unique identity. Norms, because they are ordinarily unclarified understandings, are the secret contracts or agreements of an institution. In fact, norms may hide the organization's "skeletons in the closet" collected over the course of time.

Norms provide a watershed for organizational life. If the norms are healthy, positive, and growth enhancing, ministry can be extended indefinitely. If, however, the norms are unhealthy, negative, and growth limiting, ministry may be stymied and invite decline.

There's a mystical quality about norms. They possess a strange power for conformity that's stronger than the influence of any single idea or person in the organization. A pastor, for example, once waxed eloquent in a sermon he felt strongly about. His eloquence and zeal caused the sermon to become longer than usual. He preached past twelve o'clock, the norm for the benediction in the congregation. Sensing a general restlessness among his listeners, the pastor angrily announced, "I don't care if every roast in Texas overcooks today! I'm going to finish my sermon." He finished his sermon and cooked his own goose in the process.

The congregation forgot the content of the sermon—but they never forgot the breaching of their norm. As a result, the pastor soon moved to a new church (and probably bought a new watch too). He learned how brittle and explosive congregational norms are. Like land mines, norms surprise and mutilate the unwary.

Time and scheduling are ripe areas for norms. Almost everyone has his own idea of when a committee work session should conclude, for instance. If a concluding time isn't specified, a lot of group energy may get frittered away by members fretting over the violation of their private deadlines.

 Norms are different than standards. Standards are what we say will happen; norms are what actually happens. Standards are customarily formal goals; norms are informal, but real, goals. Conflict flares when standards and norms become visibly dissimiliar.

An interim pastor discovered an illustration of the difference between norms and standards. He was moderating a business conference in a small Kentucky church in which the decision-making standard was majority rule. The little church only had twenty or thirty members present for the conference. After a hymn and a prayer, the congregation settled down to conduct its business. The interim pastor noticed a strange pattern. Even though the small congregation was seated on the left side of the center aisle, when a new issue was presented for discussion, no one would speak and all eyes would glance immediately to the right. Soon it became apparent the pianist and her husband, the only persons sitting on the right side of the church near the piano, were the objects of interest. The interim pastor observed the pianist's husband wielded so much power in the congregation that no other member would state his position until it was clear where Mr. Piano stood on the issue.

Majority voting was the standard; Mr. Piano's power was the obvi-ous decision-making norm. Standards are ideals; norms are reality.

Change and Norms

Most organizations and groups have a "tolerance zone" with-in which slight exceptions to the rules are acceptable. A small mar-gin of elasticity created by an emergency condition, an exceptional case, or a celebrity allows a little deviation from the normal.[4] A visiting seminary professor, when confronted with wearing a preaching robe for a formal worship service, demanded, "Do I have to wear this?"

"No," replied the host pastor.

"All right," relaxed the guest, "then I'll wear it!" The visiting minister wasn't used to preaching robes (his norm) and the hosting congregation was willing to be flexible (their tolerance zone) with their guest. In most organizational settings there's a clear sense of "norm-al" behavior and "ab-norm-al," or unacceptable behavior.

How then can norms be changed? Very carefully; and some-times with great difficulty. Norms are explosive. Challenging and changing congregational norms demand sensitivity, patience, timing, and skill. Some basic actions provide an approach for norm adjustment.

1. Identify the organization's norms. The early church believed a demon had to be named before it could be exorcised. The same principle holds with norms. Recognition precedes change.

2. Evaluate the norms. Judge whether they are health induc-ing.

3. Take ownership of the healthy norms. Support and use them.

4. Talk about the norm. This is often the first public action and must be done tenderly and within a pastoral relationship. Otherwise, confronting norms becomes so abrasive and escalates conflict so rapidly, resistance may become entrenched and hostile.

5. Define a new, healthier norm. Jesus' story of the demon

who returned with seven friends (Luke 11:24-26) and worsened the state of the once free man reminds us of a principle of physics: nature abhors a vacuum. Organizations don't tolerate norm vacuums either. Unless constructive alternative norms are incorporated, the organization may be worse off than before the old norms were challenged.

1 • Practice the new norm as a fresh behavioral rule for your congregation.

2 • When possible, develop a standard first. Norms aligning with standards gather the momentum of both the informal and formal systems of the organization.

3 • When possible, change healthier norms first. Sick norms are apt to be more deeply entrenched in their pathology than norms that are simply marginal.

4 • Attempt conservative change. Going back to the old way is generally an easier change approach than a radical, new one. Bishop Pike regularly introduced radical change by calling for a return to "tradition."

ACTION EXERCISE #10

Naming Our Organization's Norms

1. What are the "rules" that govern our church? Have these rules been violated? How? By whom? At what cost?
2. What do people feel free and easy doing in our church?
3. What do people "have permission" to do in our church?
4. What do people feel pressured to do in our church?
5. What have people wanted to do but felt pressured not to do in our church?

6. What have people felt pressured not to do; therefore, people don't do it and feel at ease?
7. What issues trigger conflict?

Strategies for changing norms by congregations range from safe and relatively ineffective to risky but more effective.

*   • Leaders can silently model new norms. This approach is safer but not too effective.
*   • Leaders can cause ferment by talking about unhealthy norms publicly.
*   • Groups within the congregation can support each other in confronting destructive norms.
*   • Congregations can take responsibility for examining and adjusting their own norms toward health. This approach is generally most effective, but it's also riskiest.

Examining norms may lead you to look closely at the depth of ministry your church provides. Changes may be needed for health.

Plateau: View from the Top

Organizations die on autopilot. Coasting and admiring past victories leads to organizational inertia, a plateau.[5] Since the plateau is at the apex, the institutional situation appears secure. But this quiet time in organizational life is really a lull before the storm. Soon some stakeholders may become uneasy with simply settling for the past or at the sense of being stuck; they will rock the boat.

If the ministry stage is the promise of the dream, an organizational plateau is a threat to the dream. A plateau is the forerunner of organizational disease.

A congregation is especially vulnerable to the organizational plateau after marked ministry successes or a period of growth. Several dynamics work together to create this vulnerability. The leaders may lose their personal touch as membership increases. Communication may become slower and some members or groups miss needed information. Smugness may follow a string of triumphs. The organization may multiply its policies, procedures, and paperwork. "paperalysis" or "fat paper" may bog down administrative processes in forms, reports, and requisitions that were once persons-to-person exchanges.[6] Trying simply to hold the organization's position is ignoring the storm on the horizon and inviting decline.

There are several identifying signs of the organizational plateau in a congregation.

• Inertia quietly sets in and begins to control. Tradition and history become paramount. Experimentation and change are resisted. The leadership and power structure embed themselves. A clear pecking order emerges. Conformity and dependence are valued more. The rut begins to wear deeper and deeper.

• Membership growth slows, stops, and sometimes declines.

• Programs and ministries struggle for participants.

• Giving levels and budget resources tighten. Budgets may become less flexible as debts or traditional expenditures squeeze new ministry options out.

• Member morale levels off and energy reservoirs dry up a bit.

• Available resources diminish, especially if leaders lose vision, the community changes, or the economy stagnates or reverses.

• The congregation substitutes a "franchised faith" for their dream. Some churches begin following their denomination's programs by rote when the plateau occurs. They stop adapting their denomination's suggested ministries and materials to their unique dream. Like a fast-food restaurant, these congregations begin to look and act like every other church wearing the same denominational label. The creativity and power of the dream is surrendered to franchised uniformity and loyalty.

• The organization's climate prepares to tilt subtly from healthy to unhealthy.

Not all of these occurrences happen in every church. Some plateaus are long-term while others are brief. But the ministry pace and production slow enough for the signs to be seen.

Plateau Pathologies

Physicians use diagnostic tools to name and select a course of treatment for illnesses. Churches on the plateau become sick and need diagnosis and treatment too. Note some of the church plateau pathologies listed below and their primary symptoms.[7]

• "Ethnikitis": the church isolating itself in a racially-changing community.

• "Congregational geriatrics": the church dying of old age.

• "People-blindness": the church ignoring cultural and sociological differences.

• "Hyper-cooperativism": the church choosing cooperative ministries over growth.

• "Koinonitis": the church focusing on self-serving fellowship.

• "Sociological strangulation": the church bogging down in its own success.

• Arrested spiritual development: the church undernourishing its members.

• "Saint John's syndrome": the church routinizing faith and ministry into tradition and social contact.

These pathologies and others affect the plateaued congregation. Recognizing both the plateau and the type of sickness are basic steps for the congregation that's trying to get unstuck and moving and ministering effectively again. While illness labels don't solve problems, they do provide a shorthand method of defining issues and a beginning point for discovering why the congregation's dream is in disarray.

Tilt! The Decline Begins

After the plateau phenomenon occurs in an organization, the climate shifts from healthy to unhealthy and decline begins. This tilt is ordinarily unspectacular and unobserved. In a few cases, the tilt may be triggered by some dramatic or traumatic event. More often than not, the dream slowly erodes and organizational decline blindsides a congregation.

One way to picture the tilt is to contrast a regenerative organization with a degenerative one.[8] When some critical characteristics are placed on continua from high to low, the contrast becomes clearer.

Regenerative   Degenerative
Organizations   Organizations

```
HI ← — — — — — — — TRUST — — — — — — — → Lo
Hi ← — — — — — — — OPENNESS — — — — — — → Lo
Hi ← — — — — — — STAKEHOLDING — — — — — → Lo
Lo ← — — — — EXPERIMENTATION RISK — — — — → Hi
```

While the use of the terms *regeneration* and *degeneration* refer to organizational concerns in this context, some theological implications are obvious too. Regenerative systems are dream based and oriented to planning. These organizations have momentum and can't lose for winning. Degenerative systems are doubt based and oriented to problem solving. They are bogged down in the mire of inertia and can't win for losing. A quick way to determine whether your congregation is a regenerative or degenerative organization is to observe initiative. Does your church spend its time and energy planning or problem solving? Is the initiative focus proactive or reactive?

Direction—Toward Health?

Another method of dramatizing the tilt from a regenerative to a degenerative organizational climate is to contrast unhealthy congregations and healthy ones.[9] The perfectly healthy congregation is probably too utopian for sinful human beings to maintain. Even though idealistic, a healthy congregation is moving toward health, a direction of hope rather than an accomplished state.

Unhealthy Directions	*Healthy Directions*
1. The dream is owned by an elite few.	1. The dream is owned by a broad base of members.
2. Decision making is a top-level function only.	2. Group participation in decision making is common practice.

3. During crisis members withdraw and blame each other.	3. Crisis unifies members.
4. Territory is defended.	4. Leaders invite suggestions, feedback, and critique.
5. Leaders feel isolated and act alone.	5. A team atmosphere and shared responsibility are apparent.
6. Members compete.	6. Members cooperate.
7. Personal needs are less important than organizational goals or vice versa.	7. Formal goals and personal needs are both treated as important.
8. Conflict is seen as sinful, destructive, and to be avoided.	8. Conflict is viewed as inevitable, constructive, and to be used for personal and organizational growth.
9. Innovation is surrendered to tradition.	9. Innovation and experimentation are low risk and encouraged.
10. Open disagreement is discouraged.	10. Agreement and disagreement are both acceptable and unhealthy agreement is confronted.[10]

Healthy congregations are more able to meet challenges and adapt to changes. Healthy congregations minister with their members instead of around them. Healthy congregations know who they are and where they are going.

Wanted: Visionaries and Managers

Every Christian has leadership responsibilities. As a person grasped by Jesus' dream of the kingdom of God, a Christian is responsible for implementing the dream, for ministry. Christian leadership is simply one application of the Reformation principle of the priesthood of every believer.

In my experience, churches are populated by several types of lay leaders. Each type of church member has a distictive slant on the congregation's dream and has, therefore, a slightly different sense of responsibility for the dream. The *quarterback,* the congregation's most powerful signal caller, can determine directions and goals to a significant extent. Power for the quarterback may be the result of congregational service, money, or community influence. The *legitimizers* want to be in on decision making and have sufficient influence either to bless as legitimate or block as illegitimate any program by means of their group support or opposition. Legitimizers often make up an informal inner circle for the minister and become sounding boards for his ideas.

The *lobbyists* are the special interest persons or groups within any congregation. Lobbyists are usually one-issue members who have a favorite doctrine or program they support to the virtual exclusion of all others. Some lobbyists would probably prefer to be legitimizers, but they aren't in the inner circle for some reason. The *founders* are cousins of the lobbyists. Founders are often charter members of the congregation. They are at least folk who feel and act as if they began the enterprise. In young churches, founders may be the visionaries of the congregation and lobby for the dream. Or, in older congregations founders may become rigid traditionalists who lobby for the past and against change.

The *negatives* are folk who are against everything as a matter of style and principle. They have learned being negative is often a more powerful stance in a group than being positive. However, many negatives don't have the flexibility to pick and choose their issues. They tend to be uniformly opposed to all new approaches. Sometimes negative, but always confused, is the *church neurotic.* The church neurotic either knows of a problem in the congregation or causes one. After "wolf" is cried a few times, only negatives and newcomers pay much attention to the neurotic.

The *activists* are the backbone of any congregation. They attend worship, teach classes, give time and money, visit prospects and shut-ins, sing in choirs, chaperone Youth groups, and live out their dream daily. Activists pray and participate, work and witness, lead and follow.

The *wise member* is the spiritual giant of the congregation. The wise member's judgment, counsel, and spiritual maturity are among the most precious resources of any congregation. The wise member is the person folk quickly and naturally turn to for advice and ministry when the minister is absent.

Balanced leadership is essential to church health. Whether pastors and staff or laypersons, some leaders are conceptualizers and others are operators.[11] That is, the gift of some leaders is dreaming and for others it's doing. In order for a congregation to be healthy, transforming leadership, which inspires and motivates, and transacting leadership, which manages resources, need to be present in some strength and balance.[12] Balance in ministry includes both prayer and action, both membership growth and social ministry, both evangelism and discipleship, and both reflective study and aggressive involvement.

No healthy congregation can depend solely on its pastor for its kingdom dream. Although a church's minister is a pivotal person as the congregation's most public leader, the entire congregation is responsible for church management. All the members must help direct church resources toward church goals. The pastor and staff guide the day-by-day implementation of churchwide goals and try to maintain an overall perspective of the congregation's dream and ministry.

From Here to Eternity

Ministry is what a congregation does daily because of its vision of God's kingdom. Ministry should be endless and ageless as it's empowered by the spirit of Christ. Too often, however, as churches grow and become more complex or age and become tradition bound, organizational decline sets in. Fortunately, decline in organizations can be reversed or at least minimized. Unfortunately, not every congregation is ready to dream again.

Notes

1. Lyle E. Schaller, *The Pastor and the People* (Nashville: Abingdon Press, 1973), p. 106.

2. Sam Keen, *To a Dancing God* (New York: Harper & Row, Publishers, 1970), p. 109.

3. Eliza L. DesPortes, *Congregations in Change* (New York: Seabury Press, Inc., 1973), p. 199; Edgar H. Schein, *Process Consultation* (Reading, Massachusetts: Addison-Wesley Publishing Co., Inc., 1969), pp. 59-61.

4. Jurgen Ruesch, *Knowledge in Action* (New York: Aronson, 1975), pp. 200-203.

5. George S. Ordiorne, *How Managers Make Things Happen* (Englewood Cliffs, New Jersey: Prentice-Hall, Inc., 1961), pp. 7-17; Lyle E. Schaller, *Hey, That's Our Church* (Nashville: Abingdon Press, 1975), pp. 39-50.

6. Lee Grossman, "A Manager's Approach to the Paperwork Explosion," *Management Review*, September, 1978, pp. 57-61.

7. C. Peter Wagner, *Your Church Can Be Healthy* (Nashville: Abingdon Press, 1979).

8. Adapted from Robert T. Golembiewski, *Renewing Organizations* (Itasca, Illinois: F. E. Peacock, Publishers, Inc., 1972), pp. 30-32.

9. Adapted from material by Jack K. Fordyce and Raymond Weil, *Managing WITH People* (Reading, Massachusetts: Addison-Wesley Publishing Co., Inc., 1971), pp. 11-14.

10. William G. Dyer, *Team Building* (Reading, Massachusetts: Addison-Wesley Publishing Co., Inc., 1977), p. 93 *ff.*

11. Robert K. Greenleaf, *Servant Leadership* (New York: Paulist/Newman Press, 1977), pp. 66-69, 96.

12. James MacGregor Burns, *Leadership* (New York: Harper & Row, Publishers, 1978).

Part III
The Unhealthy Congregation

8
I Remember Better Days!

We don't often see a "Condemned by Order of the City" sign tacked to the front door of a church. But I saw such a sign on the big double doors of a Southwestern Old First Church. Beside the condemned sanctuary stood a new, temporary metal building housing church offices and a worship center.

The congregation had known for years that the sanctuary was decaying. Discussions about the building's condition had been held periodically. But no decision had been made. Finally, the city government took the situation in hand and declared the building unsafe for public use. Even then the congregation couldn't face their need for either renovating or removing the old sanctuary.

I couldn't imagine what had brought Old First to such an impasse. When I asked a long-time member to explain the situation, he said sadly, "We couldn't bring ourselves to change a thing in the old building. After all, it's where Dr. So-and-So preached back when he was our pastor." The memory of former days under the ministry of a well-known pastor had paralyzed Old First's congregation. That's nostalgia.

After a congregation plateaus and the organizational balance tips toward degeneration, nostalgia appears, Nostalgia in an organizational setting is indicated by the mood, "It isn't working as well as it used to, is it?"

Nostalgia is an exile mentality.[1] Fulfillment is contingent on

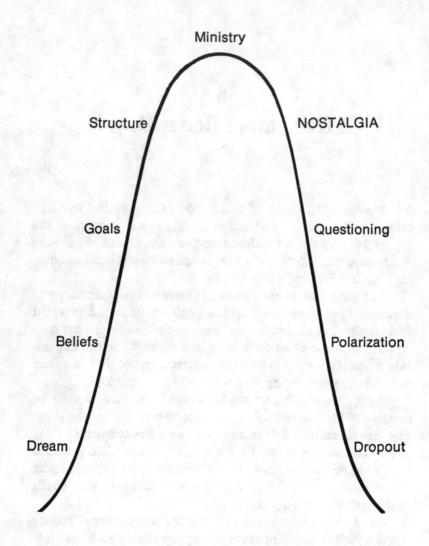

Ministry

Structure   NOSTALGIA

Goals   Questioning

Beliefs   Polarization

Dream   Dropout

the "once upon a time" remembrances of yesterday. "I remember when" stories become commonplace in organizations during nostalgic days. The golden days are remembered fondly. From an organizational perspective, nostalgia signals the beginning of a trend toward a lack of trust, unstable relationships, and an erosion of commitment to present programs and ministries.

Organizational Homesickness

Nostalgia is a current fad in America. Popular television shows and movies remind us of the less complicated, happy days of the 1940s and 1950s. An annual nostalgia convention even provides a place for Americans to display or sell old record collections, political campaign buttons, and antique cars. Simpler yesterdays are preferred to uncertain tomorrows.

The word *nostalgia* derives from two Greek words, *nostos* (to return home) and *algia* (a painful condition). Homesickness is our English word equivalent. The term was initially applied to Swiss mercenary soldiers who became despondent and melancholy while fighting in foreign lands. These soldiers became homesick for the Alps and for calmer periods of their lives.[2] Change or unpleasant circumstances trigger wistful longing for past memories in all of us.

Homesickness shows up in congregations too. The early stages of organizational decline are clearly manifested in nostalgia. A phenomenon of change, nostalgia afflicts mobile societies and organizations in transition. Nostalgia is experienced by persons "who do not like where they have arrived and have no taste for the next destination."[3]

Nostalgia in an organizational setting is the feeling of being caught betwixt and between. The future threatens; the past seems familiar and attractive; the present is uncertain enough to cause tentativeness. Congregations get mired down between their glory age and future shock. It's a frustrating time for organizational leaders to cope with.

The Many Faces of Nostalgia

Nostalgia shows several faces. Each face represents a slightly different feeling about nostalgia in persons and their institutions.

• Nostalgia longs for a return to "the good old days." As a result, contemporary America has been described as a "retread culture."[4] Re-creations, spin-offs, and remakes are the rage of the popular media.

A problem with nostalgia is its selective memory. Charles Kuralt, CBS television commentator, observes, "There are three kinds of memories—good, bad, and convenient." From a distance, our memories magnify the pleasant and shrink the unpleasant. Triumphs are romanticized and tragedies are blotted out. The blunt bottom line is: "Nostalgia selects only what is agreeable, and even that it distorts or turns into a myth."[5]

In the wise words of Will Rogers, "Things ain't what they used to be and probably never was." I've experienced an example of nostalgia's selective memory. I was born several years after the Depression of the 1930s. But I remember my family and others speaking warmly of how closely knit families were and how close to God people became during the Depression. Their wistful tones implied if another depression came, families would stabilize and religion revive.

To check out the realities of the Depression, I reviewed several hours of old theater newsreels from the thirties. The poverty and desperation of the era were obvious. But the "campfire stories" told years later had a much more generous slant. So, we nostalgically recall the 1930s with little of the economic hardships, the 1940s with little bloodshed from World War II, the 1950s without the witch-hunts of McCarthyism, the 1960s without Vietnam, and the 1970s without Watergate.

Nostalgia hungers for the way we were. But the "good old days" probably weren't really ever that pleasant—except through the filters of selective memories.

• Nostalgia weakens our commitments to the present. This

fact is a huge threat to declining congregations. Nostalgia leaves minimal energy for today. For example, rather than do direct evangelism in today's challenging contexts, some congregations build brush arbors and stage open-air revivals.

It's always tempting to give allegiance to the past. While struggling with terminal cancer, political optimist Hubert H. Humphrey evaluated yesterday's good old days in a televised interview: "They were never that good, believe me. The good new days are today, and better days are coming tomorrow. Our greatest songs are still unsung."

In nostalgic moments, it's tough to remember yesterday is dead and tomorrow is blind. Rather, we select one or the other and cop out on today. Organizations fall into "if only" syndromes and consider turning back to better times instead of renewing their dream and forging new ministry initiatives.

• Nostalgia provides a fragile bridge to the future. In a more positive light, continuity between past and future is provided by nostalgia.

Upheaval triggers nostalgic periods of history. Review the past half century of American history—Depression, World War II and the bomb, Korea and the Cold War, Vietnam, political assassinations, Watergate, inflation. It's easy to see why moderns wish for easier options, a slower pace, and a happier era in which to live. We need emotionally to repeat some good old days. Nostalgia lends a sense of psychological stability, an oasis in history. Nostalgia gives us a toehold on turbulence.

A retreat into a "safe" past may remind us of our roots and allow a foray into the future. Nostalgia is proof of our past. And the past is our stepping-stone into tomorrow.

While in the death camp of Auschwitz, psychiatrist Victor Frankl experienced the past-present-future link nostalgia provides. Amid the cold, sickness, emotional desolation, and spiritual poverty of the holocaust, Frankl thought back: "In my mind I took bus rides, unlocked the front door of my apartment, answered my telephone, switched on the electric lights. Our thoughts often centered on such details, and these memories could move one to tears.'' Then one night a fellow prisoner passed the word to the tired and hungry inmates of a spectacular sunset. Everyone quickly went outside and silently absorbed the colors and shapes of the clouds. Finally, a prisoner broke the silence, 'How beautiful the world *could* be!'"[6] Such experiences provide continuity in our lives and the courage to go forward.

In summary, nostalgia wears at least three faces of importance to organizations.

• Successes, real or selected, can seduce a congregation into only looking backward. Prochnow counseled: "Forget the past. No one becomes successful in the past." That sentiment is half-true. We can learn from the past. But we can't live in it.

• Nostalgia's second face limits loyalty to the present. This phenomenon is a threat and challenge to the kingdom dream and to organizational planning. Unless energy can be found for the present, the future dream of a congregation may become a nightmare.

• Celebrating the past can, on occasion, provide the historical continuity for risking a confrontation with the future. For this reason, temporary retreats into the past in events like homecomings and special recognitions of long-time leaders can help bridge the past-present-future link we face constantly in a rapidly changing world.

For example, a Lutheran church on the urban fringe of a Texas city suddenly found itself changing from a quiet, rural congregation into a dynamic, growing suburban church. It outgrew its small, traditional building. A building committee was appointed and, after study, recommended a modernistic architectural style for its new building. The building committee was aware of two mindsets—traditional and progressive—about equally represented in this changing congregation. As a result, they designed a small chapel-prayer room into the new structure that was a miniature of the old sanctuary. Oldtimers found this familiar spot a nostalgic retreat as many other facets of the church's ministry and program changed around them. A sense of physical continuity helped this congregation celebrate its past and journey into its future.

Nostalgia as Corporate Depression

But change can be upsetting to congregations. What depression is to individuals, nostalgia can be for organizations. Depression in persons is often triggered by anger or loss. We become angry when our institutions grow so complex they seem unmanageable. Then, since we can't confront a huge organization very directly, our anger turns inward, and we beat ourselves down emotionally. Or, we feel a loss of control over our lives when bureaucratic problems become so large and tangled we can't unravel them. Again, our futility turns within, and we become depressed. In fact, the level of morale can sink and the emotional tone of an entire organization can depress.

Tennyson noted, "Tears rise in the heart . . . thinking of the days that are no more." Congregations need to grieve too on occasion. But since grief is especially difficult to express in group settings, congregations can feel corporate depression and express it as nostalgia.[7] Then the past is glorified, and there's little energy for the present.

I once observed a stark example of organizational depression in a church where I was a member. Our pastor resigned after several years of successful ministry. A couple of weeks after he left an important leader election was held. The election was a fiasco. First, there was a very light vote. Second, the vote was so scattered that no clear consensus developed. Third, when the persons who had garnered several votes were asked to serve, many refused. Those who agreed to serve had little enthusiasm for their future tasks. Taken together, these reactions finally brought the congregation to the realization of its collective grief and depression. The church agreed to set the election aside, face our grief until it was resolved, and then resume our ministries. In retrospect, it appears the congregation made a mature decision. Soon the depression ran its course; the congregation expressed its grief and began its ministry efforts again healthily.

How can a congregation deal with corporate depression? If the example just cited can be treated as a case study, three guidelines appear. First, this congregation realized depression is generally cyclical. After they recognized they were mired in corporate depression, they admitted the depression would pass in time. Second, they vented their pent-up feelings of confusion, frustration, and anger over "abandonment" by the former pastor. The church leaders met and explored the situation first. Then, they staged a forum in which congregational grief and depression were discussed openly. The interim pastor also preached a sermon on coping with the loss of a group's primary public leader. Third, just as therapists recommend exercise for their depressed clients, this congregation began actively planning for its future journey toward its kingdom dream.

The underlying dynamic in conquering corporate depression is raising a congregation's image of itself and its confidence level. Transactional analysts refer to this action as raising the "stroke economy" of an organization.[8] Nostalgia can help the process of stroking and building confidence by deliberately reviewing past successes as a springboard for new ventures in ministry.

Making New Meanings

Ministers and other leaders help their organizations create new meanings. While the gospel message doesn't change, we are constantly forced to make new applications of it. Christianity is always only one generation away from extinction. If we ever fail to meet new challenges for ministry during a single generation, the church will become a religious dinosaur.

Visualize two streets intersecting at your church. One street carries the traditions—biblical, theological, denominational, and geographical—of your church. Traditions are the ways we've done ministry in the past. We get nostalgic over our traditions.

The second street carries the contemporary challenges for ministry—changing life-styles and values, shifting family patterns, drugs and other forms of chemical abuse, an increased interest in leisure, an aging national population, and similar concerns. These issues present opportunities for congregations to evangelize, teach, and interpret the gospel to secular minds.

These two streets symbolically meet at the church. Whether this meeting is a head-on collision or two-way traffic depends in large part on how able we are in applying our kingdom dream to contempory life situations. Jesus depicted the process of making new meanings for a group in the Sermon on the Mount. Repeatedly, he spoke of the truths said "by them of old time" and then confronted them with new ministry applications in his "but I say unto you" challenges. Making new ministry meanings from the base of the old message is a creative leadership opportunity for every generation of ministers. Finding and expressing these new meanings is an alternative to lounging in nostalgia.

ACTION EXERCISE #11

Measuring Our Church's Nostalgia Quotient

1. Of how many different events, persons, or concerns can I imagine members of our congregation saying, "I remember when . . .?"
2. What ministries, programs, or practices would our congregation be talking about if they said, "It isn't working as well as it used to, is it?"
3. Which eras of our congregation's history are remembered warmly and often?

Ministering in the Nostalgic Church

Corporate nostalgia makes unique demands on leaders. Several guidelines are helpful in facing the nostalgic congregation creatively.

• Nostalgic church members provide an early warning system

of organizational decline. The presence of persistent and wide-spread nostalgia is a signal that decline has begun and revitalization measures must be applied.

• Nostalgic members are usually friendly toward leaders. Their wistfulness and longing for the past grows out of their traditionalism. They are the conservators of old victories, but they can remind leaders organizational slippage is in process.

• Leaders are often threatened by nostalgia. When the inevitable allusions to the past are made during nostalgic periods, leaders must protect themselves emotionally against comparisons that feel unfavorable. After all, nostalgia is an organizational phenomenon, not an individual attack. In a former church, a fire had occurred during a congregational growth boom. While the burned building was rebuilt, the church worshiped in a tent. One Easter over nine hundred people gathered under the tent for worship. Although ten years had passed since that all-time high attendance record had been set, members would speak longingly of the fire, the tent, and over nine hundred worshiping in the tent. Since many fewer attended the church during my era, I often felt threatened by references to the fire and its aftermath. In my fantasies, I sometimes was tempted to burn down the building again and rent a tent for our return to the glory days!

• Nostalgia is an emotionally cool phase of organizational life. The longing and the wistful sentiments are not angry yet. From the viewpoint of transactional analysis, the three ego states shift as a congregation moves around the health cycle from stage to stage.[9] Leaders need to act to revitalize a nostalgic institution before cool emotions heat up.

• Nostalgia, taken in strictly organizational terms, is a doubting of structure. The temptation is to restructure, often a cosmetic strategy for organizational renewal. Restructure's new look may yield a brief surge of energy and favorable response. But, to really remedy nostalgia, the organization's goals should be examined and reshaped. The structure nostalgia remembers so fondly may no longer represent the current goals of the church.

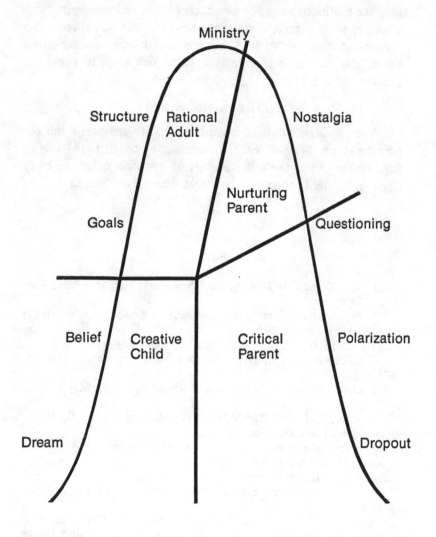

• A major task of the leader of a nostalgic organization is to keep the traditions *versus* contemporary issues dialogue open. Nostalgia, to some degree, always represents the tension between who we are and where we've been. Momentum for new ministry grows out of shared meanings as members find new ways to apply the gospel to life.

Lull Before the Storm

The nostalgia phase of organizational life provides a lull before the storm. Steeper decline and escalating conflict are likely to follow. Therefore, the relative quiet of nostalgia offers an early signal of the need for an initiative toward congregational health.

Notes

1. Sam Keen, *To a Dancing God* (New York: Harper & Row, Publishers, 1970), pp. 7-8.

2. Fred Davis, *Yearning for Yesterday: a Sociology of Nostalgia* (New York: Free Press, 1979), p. 1.

3. "Past Shock," *New York Times Magazine*, May 4, 1975, p. 6.

4. "The Retread Culture," *New York Times Magazine*, October 26, 1975, p. 38.

5. Gerald Clarke, "The Meaning of Nostalgia," *Time*, May 3, 1971, p. 77.

6. Victor E. Frankl, *Man's Search for Meaning* (New York: Washington Square Press, 1963), pp. 61-63.

7. A case of national depression in political concerns is documented by Alexander and Margarete Mitscherlich, *The Inability to Mourn: Principles of Collective Behavior* (New York: Grove Press, 1975).

8. Claude M. Steiner, *Scripts People Live* (New York: Grove Press, 1974), pp. 323-334.

9. This application is implied by Roger Kaufman, "Organizational Improvement: a Review of Models and an Attempted Synthesis," *Group and Organization Studies*, Vol. 1, No. 4, December, 1976, pp. 474-495.

9
Descent into Organizational Hell[1]

Lowell Thomas, the famous journalist, overreacted to a news story when he was a cub reporter. In his autobiography, *Good Evening Everybody,* Thomas tells of returning home to Cripple Creek, Colorado, as a brand-new college graduate and taking a newspaper job. When a town fire occurred, Thomas used a huge typeface usually reserved for posters and handbills and ran the headline, Blaze Sweeps Local Buildings!

An old newspaperman observed what Lowell Thomas was about to do and asked, "Exactly how many buildings burned?

"Three," replied Thomas a bit sheepishly.

"I'll tell you what, kid," drawled the seasoned journalist. "I'd try to hold something back for the second coming!"

Declining congregations are prone toward seeing disaster looming on the horizon. Every evidence of hastening decline touches off our organizational "catastrophe reflex." Questioning, polarization, and apathy are best described by two words—worse and faster. Organizationally, the congregational climate will decay rapidly during the descent into conflict.

The Fright of Church Fights

Many church members are frightened of and disappointed by conflict. We may welcome competition in athletics and tolerate

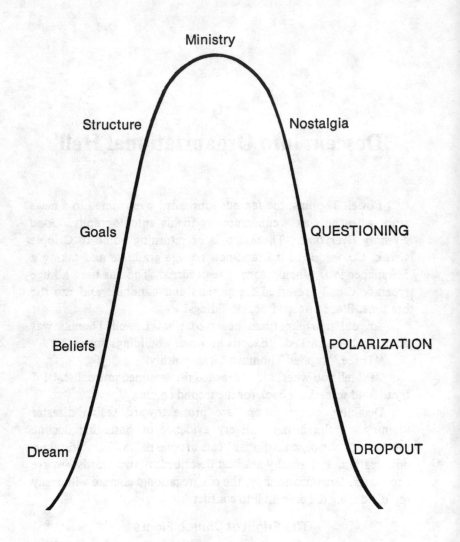

cutthroat tactics in the marketplace, but we're scared of conflict in the church.

There are several reasons why we Christians don't like conflict in our congregations. (1) We expect the church to be a community of reconciliation and wholeness. In spite of the fact that conflict is a natural phenomenon which can be handled constructively, we're afraid conflict will be divisive and weaken the congregation's witness and image in the community. (2) Some people feel conflict is unchristian. We may expect all Christians to believe the same doctrines at the same level of commitment and act on our convictions by supporting the same ministries. But to feel Christians never disagree is to overlook the rich differences between persons and denominations.

(3) We may never have experienced the power of the negative. Several years ago I read Edgar Schein's assertion that three positive statements were needed to offset one negative statement in working groups.[2] In other words, a negative response is three times as powerful as an affirming word.

I had often seen an angry outburst or a speech of opposition freeze a group's ability to act. I decided to test Schein's observation. During a role-play session in a training lab, I waited silently until our mock church staff reached a decision and then verbally attacked the man playing the pastor's role. My verbal assault had two results: the decision was reversed and the pastor never spoke again during the role playing. I discovered being against something can be a heady stance. Now I understand one reason why some folk are characteristically opposed to whatever is happening in their congregations. "It'll never fly, Wilbur" is generally heard with more impact than "Amen, Brother."

Whether we like conflict or not, it's here to stay—even in the church. And as a congregation declines, it becomes more prone to various aspects of conflict.

Level 1: Questioning

If the concerns of nostalgic members are ignored, the organization soon moves deeper into decline. Serious questioning begins.

The tone of the inquiries changes to doubt, irritability, and anger. The goals of the organization come under fire. The content of questioning focuses on, Is this the right goal for our church? Are we on the right track? Should our church provide this ministry? Casual responses or the denominational party line answers aren't adequate any longer. To say, "Baptists (or Catholics or Jews) have always done ministry like this," or, "Nashville (or New York or Philadelphia) recommends this approach" isn't sufficient reason to convince the serious questioner.

Without direct and effective organizational revitalization measures, the crisis is set. The point of no return has been reached. Either the conflict will be resolved or at least managed at the questioning level or it may destroy the organization. Questioning is the now-or-never point of congregational health. Health or death are the choices.

Signs of questioning appear in members' behaviors. An executive of a declining company describes the organizational death-watch process he observed as his business died.

> When a complex organization begins to fall apart, it doesn't go all at once: it isn't like a bomb in the cellar or a plane crash. It happens in bits and pieces, a fissure here, a missing part there.
>
> The process starts with the people. They become angry. Or frightened. Or restless. They take longer lunches. They change their work habits; those who worked long hours now work less; those who took it easy begin to show up on time and leave later. They talk a lot about the man at the top.[3]

The questioning stage of congregational life indicates deepening organizational disease. Questioning is the "last chance" level for new life and ministry.

Level 2: Polarization

If the organizational response to questioning is inadequate, the sense of doubt intensifies and polarization occurs. While a great deal of congregational conflict is triggered by personality clashes in their varied guises, battle lines can also be drawn along doctrinal or ethical lines. The "Is this right?" questions of the previous stage are now answered with strongly emotional yeses and noes. Some members respond with conviction: "No! That isn't right! It's wrong! We can't 'do church' like that any longer." Other members are just as vigorous in answering, "Yes! We must continue to 'do church' like that!"

Conflict is now open, escalating, and messy. "We" *versus* "they," "this" as opposed to "that," "right" or "wrong" issues become rampant. As polarization wedges congregational factions apart, churches may divide or at least immobilize their influences and ministries both within and beyond their membership.

How conflict is viewed shapes the basis for dealing with congregational polarization. Your assumptions regarding conflict determine your coping strategies.[4]

• Conflict indicates a basic relationship. It takes enormous energy to disagree or fight with others. When we engage in conflict with other persons, we generally have a fairly strong relationship with them. In other words, church fights are rarely between strangers. Conflict shows enough caring to expend the energy and time necessary for dealing with our differences.

• Close relationships create more threatening conflict. There's more at stake in conflict when friendships as well as issues are involved. Additionally, intimates know where their opponent's weaknesses and sore spots are. On the other side, the sense of being betrayed by a friend escalates disagreement into fury. This dynamic causes many church fights to degenerate into personality clashes in which the primary "facts" of the conflict are the negative feelings of persons.

• High ownership means keener conflict. Stakeholders are generally the principals in organizational conflict. Church conflict is especially volatile because it deals with religion, a core value, an emotional concern of members. When people feel strongly about an issue, conflict tends to be sharper.

Sometimes fringe members are drawn into church fights. Even if they haven't been deeply involved in the congregation's life immediately before polarization occurs, the conflict offers them an opportunity to "buy in" again. Reentry of fringe members into the mainstream of congregational conflict doesn't always indicate an interest in the specific issue of the conflict. Occasionally, a conflict serves as a catalyst for a variety of old disagreements and offers a stackpole around which general opposition can be expressed. Conflict has a magnetic quality in certain settings and situations.

• Group conflict introduces sharper disagreement. Two people have arguments. But two groups can start a war. Groups idealize their positions and make all issues black-and-white polarities. Where an individual may recognize his motives are mixed, groups diffuse motives and encourage a righteous attitude toward their stance. "They" becomes the enemy, in other words.

• Stable congregations have more frequent, but smaller conflicts. Healthy congregations recognize that differences enrich them. But where the "lid is kept on," pressure builds up and major decisions become battlegrounds. Polarization often occurs when only one major conflict is brewing and the members have suppressed conflict in the past. They, therefore, have little experience in dealing with conflict, and the church may lack a forum where different views can be explored openly. Stable congregations deal with their differences as they occur.

• Gunnysacking leads to dangerous conflict. When a congregation suppresses conflicts, it gunnysacks or stores them up. Finally, the sack of conflicts overflows and a major explosion occurs. As mentioned before, conflict involves enormous energy. When that energy is bottled up rather than managed, pressure can build to a dangerous level. Healthy congregations stay up-to-date on managing their conflicts. Small conflicts are easier to resolve and are less threatening to the congregation's dream.

Polarization generally creates an unhealthy atmosphere in a congregation. It indicates conflict hasn't been dealt with early and resolved constructively. As polarization deepens, the gulf between persons and groups widens. If people elect to remain in the same congregation with people they disagree with, energies may be used primarily to oppose each other. When this phenomenon occurs, ministry is diseased and weakened.

Level 3: Dropout

Apathy is the result of an organization remaining unresponsive to the nostalgia and differences of members. In the face of a "who cares?" congregational climate, some members give up and drop out. No longer do they have the energy to struggle for change. Or, they are completely disillusioned by the depth of hostility often demonstrated amid polarization. As a result, they feel nothing deeply either pro or con about the congregation. They cease to be stakeholders. Their alienation toward the organization is total, and, perhaps, final. For them the kingdom dream has died in this church setting.

A recent study of the 80 million unchurched Americans by Russell Hale describes eight major categories of persons outside organized religion: True Unbelievers, Publicans, Boxed-In, Burned-Out, Locked-Out, Nomads, Anit-Institutionalists, and Pilgrims.[5] The Burned-Out person is a church dropout. Although persons in this group were once heavily involved in congregational life, they wore down and exited. For one reason or another, they felt depleted and decided against such an intense level of church participation. One mark of an unhealthy congregation is a few persons carrying too heavy a load of organizational work. They quickly become candidates for religious burn-out.

My studies show only about one church in ten making any concerted effort to recover its dropout members. Several reasons may explain apparent disinterest in dropouts. First, church leaders may assume dropouts are hostile. That sometimes isn't the case. Quite likely their anger is spent. In fact, their lack of feeling for their church may indicate a complete breach of emotional loyalty. Second, some leaders may not realize how vast a reservoir of potential ministry volunteers is resting dormant on the fringes of their church. In a denomination-wide survey, Southern Baptists recently discovered 27 percent of their numbers were actually inactive church members.[6] When over one in four members aren't participating in or contributing to the ministries of their own congregations, many human resources are being wasted.

Differences in Decline

In summary, the descent into organizational hell is an uncomfortable time in a congregation's life. Pain is caused by the escalating intensity and pace of conflict. Some subtle, but crucial, differences occur as the church cycles from questioning to polarization to dropping out. First, the polarization and drop out phenomena signal a switch back to the more intuitive and emotional right brain hemisphere.

Second, to use an ethical parallel, the questioning level is akin to the social change strategy of civil disobedience. Where civil disobedience is practiced, there is still a basic loyalty to the institution even though questions of right and wrong are being raised. Energies are still flowing into the organization because of a commitment to it. But at the polarization stage, important changes happen. Now rebellion is possible and likely because many participant's loyalties are no longer pledged to the institution. These members are linked to the organization mostly by anger. Then, at the dropout level, persons have moved beyond revolution. If these persons have any energy for organizational life, it will be focused on a new dream. If their old dream has died, they probably won't have energy to resurrect it. Many, of course, will simply coast along completely outside institutionalized religious life.

Variance Sensors—Resource Persons for Revitalization

One result of conflict is many quality Christians move to the fringes of the congregation. They are half in and half out of the ministry mainstream. There they join other members who because of health or burn-out pressures are also fringe members.

Some fringe members are variance sensors.[7] Variance sensors are usually members who have been active formerly and have participated in the congregation over a long period of time. At present they are basically loyal to the church but are primarily observers of the church's life. They understand the dream of the congregation and can sense when the direction of the church is at variance from the dream.

The variance sensor is a valuable resource for church leaders. These loyal members aren't ready to reenlist in the fray, but when approached they will usually offer counsel and encouragement to leaders who are trying to facilitate the dreaming process. Variance sensors are willing to make observations from behind the scenes but aren't yet willing to accept leadership responsibility again. Informal guidance is the primary resource from variance sensors. But even informal suggestions from persons who understand the difference between dreaming and drifting are invaluable.

Conflict may leave the congregation's visionaries inactive. It's possible for much of the spiritual strength of a church to be left in an observer's role after a church fight.

Notes

1. The chapter title is parallel to an affirmation in the Apostles' Creed: "He descended into hell."

2. Edgar H. Schein, *Process Consultation* (Reading, Massachusetts: Addison-Wesley Publishing Co., Inc., 1969), p. 18.

3. Rosabeth Moss Kanter and Barry A. Stein (eds.), *Life in Organizations: Workplaces as People Experience Them* (New York: Basic Books, Inc., 1979), p. 377.

4. Speed Leas and Paul Kittlaus, *Church Fights: Managing Conflict in the Local Church* (Philadelphia: Westminster Press, 1973), pp. 43-48.

5. "Looking from the Inside Out," *Time*, October 3, 1977, p. 85.

6. Lewis Wingo, "Where Are All Those Non-resident Members?" *Quarterly Review*, April-May-June, 1976, pp. 68-71. For an illustration of one congregation's efforts to deal with its dropouts, see Sanford R. Beckett, "Ministering to Nonresident Church Members," *Search*, Spring, 1979, pp. 14-23.

7. Warren Bennis, *The Unconscious Conspiracy: Why Leaders Can't Lead* (New York: AMACOM, 1976), p. 63. Another type of variance sensor is the active member who is a good problem identifier. They are generally under fire from other members who prefer to avoid problems and think positively all the time.

Part IV
Awakening a Healthy Dream

10
Dreaming Again!

A friend of mine suggests a powerful sequence within institutional life: from a man to a movement to a machine to a monument. His observation is correct. Organizations are more likely to be dynamic and healthy when they're new. The second generation of institutional leaders may not carry on the founding dream. They may settle for oiling the machine and maintaining the monument.

Some congregations inadvertently choose to maintain themselves and simply survive. Others dream and plan. Dreaming and planning is the healthier option. This chapter suggests some ways the dreaming process can be implemented. Let's begin with an actual case, the young Lakeside Church.

Good Start or Bad Dream?

Lakeside Church had a healthy and happy history. At five years old, the congregation numbered nearly six hundred members. Located in a planned city on a South Carolina lake, the community residents around Lakeside Church are mostly Protestant, middle-aged, and financially successful. But not all was well with the congregation.

Lakeside Church had its birth in the spontaneous dream of providing worship experiences for persons living in the growing development. Two couples organized an Easter worship service for April 22, 1973. The pastor of a nearby church preached. Over two hundred persons gathered around tables on a terrace overlooking the water.

The successful Easter service concluded with an announcement. Three days later there would be a meeting of persons who wanted to explore the possibility of beginning a church. Over twenty-five people met. They organized a steering committee of five men and six women to arrange worship services for a four-month trial period. Informally, several key actions quickly occurred. A bank account was opened with the deposit of a donation. An organ was loaned to the committee. All sixty-one families who lived in the Lakeside development at that time were notified by telephone about the plans for future worship services. A polling of Lakeside's residents showed keen interest in a church, including Bible study as well as worship.

After the four-month trial period of worship services was concluded successfully in August, the budding congregation took a formal step. They elected co-moderators. Worship continued, and discussion about developing a Sunday School and budget began. The steering committee also began looking for a building site.

In October a Sunday School was organized. Christmas Eve 1973 saw a high experience of worship. (Easter and Christmas Eve continue as special times of worship at Lakeside.)

By early 1974, the growing group outlined some plans for calling a pastor. During the spring of 1974, the little church floundered amid its own disorganization. A consultant helped the steering committee develop some specific plans. These plans yielded another significant step. On August 4, 1974, a pastor selection committee was formed and immediately began searching for a full-time minister.

In the providence of God, a young minister in North Carolina was dreaming of a church like Lakeside. By December the search committee and the young minister had met, talked, and arranged a trial sermon. During the trial sermon, an illustration regarding a storm was used. Coincidently, a storm blew across the lake at that very moment. After the sermon, the search committee humorously told the young minister that no one would dare vote against him after the storm blew in on cue! The call vote was strongly affirmative and on May 15, 1975, Lakeside had its first full-time pastor on the field.

The pastor immediately began a series of sermons and discussions to clarify the theological roots of this emerging congregation. One doctrinal position was central: Jesus Christ is Lord of all of life. Additionally, the concept of the church centered on two ideas—the church gathered for worship and renewal and scattered for mission and ministry.

These sermons produced two important results. One, a covenant of the faith and dream of this group emerged.[1] The covenant was accepted by the congregation in September. The covenant beautifully affirmed the corporate beliefs of the group:

The Covenant

We believe in God the Father, Creator and creative,
He gives us His steadfast love,
shares with us our joy,
and sustains us in our suffering.
His power is open to us. We trust Him.
We follow Jesus Christ, Son of God and Son of Man.
His death becomes our victory,
His resurrection is our hope.
In Him the Word has become flesh.
In Him we are offered
forgiveness from sin,
renewal from failure,
reconciliation from brokenness,
release from despair.
We are guided by the Holy Spirit, God's presence in the world.
By the Spirit we are called into Christ's Church:
to celebrate His love,
to seek justice and resist evil.

to proclaim Jesus, crucified and risen,
to share with Him in baptism and eat at His table.
Because we are His Disciples, His pilgrim people, we joyfully
covenant with each other
to walk together in love,
to pray for one another,
to care for one another,
to live in *koinonia*.
In life, in death, in life beyond death
God is with us.
We are not alone.
Thanks be to God!
Amen.

Two, using the covenant, a call was issued for charter members. On October 5, 1975, one hundred fifty Christians declared their faith, and Lakeside Church became a reality. The dream had come true.

Or had it? Two events upset the congregation. A fire wiped out the congregation's office and Sunday School space. The search for a permanent building site was met with repeated frustration.

But a new site was finally located and purchased. Bids on a building were taken. On August 22, 1976, ground was broken, and on May 22, 1977, a new multiuse facility was dedicated.

During the next two and one-half years success followed success. The congregation grew to more than 550 members. Worship, music, and drama ministries flourished. However, growth brought its own looming specter. The new members did not understand the dream. Frustration began to simmer.

Back to the Dream

But the minister read his congregation correctly. Even at the young age of six years, his congregation was plateauing and tilting toward nostalgia. He devised a year-long, seven-event plan to redream the dream.

First, a four-month period in early 1979 was used to recall the mileposts in Lakeside's faith journey. The church's early stages were reviewed by older members in worship testimonies.

Second, a sermon series focused on the doctrine of the church in the congregation's covenant. These sermons were a review for older members and an orientation for newer ones.

Third, a new church member training program was established. It focused on the dream and made involvement in the church's ministries easier and more natural.

Fourth, a two-week Christian festival of the arts was held. More than two hundred members shared their creative, spiritual gifts through music, painting, drama, and puppetry.

Fifth, the missions committee involved a larger number of members in direct witness. Four new projects were developed and carried out.

Sixth, four sermons on the parables, coupled with four dramatic presentations on these parables, were designed to awaken in the hearers the kingdom dream of Jesus. The tension between service and "serve-us" was spotlighted.

Seventh, fifty adult church members, including most of the church council and committee chairpersons, met in a retreat center to evaluate the church's purpose and progress. Broader ownership of the kingdom dream resulted.

Dream Come True

Was reawakening the dream worth the effort for Lakeside? Yes. The two months following the completion of these seven events saw a new growth spurt with one hundred new members joining. The pastor sensed a new focus in his own ministry. Congregational morale heightened. Lakeside's dream came true again in early 1980.

Without attempting an exhaustive overview of dreaming strategies, consider some selected approaches for dreaming again at three levels of congregational life.

Consciousness Raising: Publicizing the Dream

Some aspects of awakening a dream are appropriate for total congregational settings. Worship is the most obvious public arena for proclaiming the dream and raising the consciousness of the entire congregation. Several proclamation strategies can be used to define and undergird a congregation's kingdom dream.

• Preach a sermon series on the parables. This series could extend the dreaming process and show how contemporary congregations can become "like the kingdom." For example, the precious pearl (Matt. 13:45-46) could illustrate the dimension of sacrifice and risk inherent when we become like the kingdom. Again, the mustard seed shows the potential of kingdom growth in its small-to-large contrast.

• Another preaching possibility is a health cycle sermon series (or even several short sermon series over a longer period of time). Let me suggest an outline of this approach.

In this case, a cluster of sermons on the parables could flesh out the dream stage. The belief stage could take several shapes. Lakeside Church wrote its own covenant. Beliefs could also be solidified by taking selected favorite congregational hymns which undergird the dream and building worship services around them.

The goals stage might focus sermons on "Jesus Helped Others." Since goals grow out of beliefs and dreams, an effort should be made to show how Jesus' kingdom dream expressed itself concretely in specific ministry events.

Structure could be illustrated by the "Shape of the Early Church," a sermon series on the pastoral epistles. The pastorals give clues about the way the first congregations began to structure their lives and work for implementing the kingdom dream.

The ministry stage could focus on Acts, especially the range of missionary and ministry actions the emerging church took to extend its ministry. Evangelism, fellowship, nurture, benevolence, confronting cultural barriers, and foreign missions are a few concrete elements of how diverse the church of Acts was in its practice of ministry. The series might arrange itself around the theme, "Scattered to Incarnate Christ."

"Temptations to Turn Back" might explore the nostalgia stage. The post-Exodus wilderness wanderings and the "early retirement" of the Thessalonian Christians suggest themes which illustrate how nostalgia short-circuits ministry energies.

Obviously, six brief series of sermons would focus members' attention on congregational health concerns for an extended period of time. As much as a year, excluding seasonal themes and special issues, might be needed in this approach. Ministers and other leaders would have to decide if an effort of this magnitude is a project they want to undertake.

• Structured testimonies in worship give individual members a way to express their dream for the congregation. In the worship setting, visionary laypersons can share their dream for their congregation. Focus can be built into their testimonies by asking them to complete this sentence: "Five years from now, I hope our church will be. . . ." These testimonies could be designed into ordinary worship services as vision stretching exercises. Or, a larger portion of a service could be given to impromptu testimonies with the intent of showing the breadth of vision in a church. In either case, the focus should be on the future and on enlarging concrete ministry actions implied by the dream.

Consensus Building: Support for the Dream

Congregations are also made up of classes and small groups in which the dream can be clarified and consensus developed. Small clusters of members lend themselves to personal encouragement and congregational health purposes. A range of possibilities fit small groups.

• If the small group is an educational setting, Jesus' parables can be taught. To prepare for teaching the parables, ask yourself these four interpretive questions:
1) What's the main point of this parable?
2) Who's being addressed and under what circumstances?

3) What are the comparisons and/or contrasts being made?
4) What must I do now as a faith response to this parable?

The parables create tensions in their comparisons and contrasts which help define a kingdom dream. Recently I taught the kingdom stories with special attention to these tensions.

> Old and New (Luke 5:36-39)
> Small and Large (Luke 13:18-21)
> Festivity and Faithfulness (Matt. 22:1-14)
> Planning and Piety (Luke 14:28-33)
> Lost and Found (Luke 15)
> Neighbor Need and Christian Care (Luke 10:29-37)
> Riches and Rewards (Luke 16:19-31)
> Prayers and Parade (Luke 18:9-14)

• The systemic theology information (in ch. 2 and the appendixes) could be studied and discussed in small groups. Again, the concentration of such a study would be on how the body of Christ can live out a kingdom dream.

• Exploring our own spiritual roots is an important process. For example, each person in a small group could draw and share his spiritual family tree. This drawing would trace his individual spiritual heritage. A second stage of mapping spiritual pilgrimages would develop a composite family tree for the congregation at large. Such an interpretive document would help a group examine the spiritual roots which can nourish their corporate dream.

Commitment Deepening: Leadership for the Dream

Leaders of any enterprise must be especially clear about and committed to their purposes. As leaders become clearer about shared dreams, they commit themselves more deeply to those dreams.

• The church staff and the elected leaders of church groups can go on planning retreats and examine the congregation's dream. The Hillwood Church used a simple approach for gathering members' opinions on ministries and programs. The staff asked members to write down what they felt the highs and lows of the previous year's ministry were. Then they asked members to note their hopes and fears for the next year. In a planning retreat these pluses and minuses were listed on large charts headed *Last Year* and *Next Year*. This visual comparison showed how the members at large felt about the congregation's progress toward their dream.

Also using the members' reports, Hillwood's staff proposed a theme or motto for the next year. For example, the themes for three years indicate their sense of progress: "Let's Turn Things Around" (1974), "Growing Up in Every Way" (1975), and "Let Us Go On" (1976). These mottoes gave them a shorthand way to express and keep focused on their dream.

• Old First used a series of Sunday evenings for congregational "town meetings." The first session or two centered on dreaming about many possibilities. After a number of specific interests began to revolve around the core dream, discussion groups were formed around these issues. These ten or fifteen groups suggested ministry possibilities which were later taken to the entire congregation for consideration and implementation.

Dare to Dream

Methods vary for awakening a dream. But the dynamic remains constant: vision makes the difference in a congregation. Edward Lindaman encourages us to dream: "It helps to realize that *everything that is now possible was at one time impossible.* In every case someone somewhere dared to dream, dared to imagine something a little better, a little different."[2] A dream defined and owned can change your church. Ultimately, your dream might change our planet.

Notes

1. Gene Jester, "Building a Church from a Dream," (unpublished D.Min. project report, Southeastern Baptist Theological Seminary, 1980), p. 103.

2. Edward B. Lindaman, *Thinking in the Future Tense* (Nashville: Broadman Press, 1978), p. 44.

11
Planning for Vitality

"Ninety percent of baseball is mental. The other half is physical," claims Yogi Berra. Yogi's math is a bit off, but his statement applies accurately to dreaming and planning. The dream, the mental work, comes first and requires a lot of effort. The rest of the revitalization process is planning and doing—the physical work. After the dream, we simply plan our work and work our plans.

Congregational planning describes the actions taken to move from dreaming to doing ministry. The essential movements of a planning process can be diagrammed:

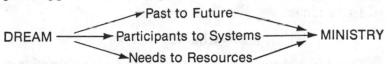

Planning is dynamic movement, not mechanical methods. Planning links vision to implementation.

Planning for ministry involves three basic advances.

• Movement from past to future. Planning provides continuity for the movement from history to the future. We can't change our pasts. Our yesterdays provide a foundation for our tomorrows.

The future forces us to anticipate. We in the church must become futurists and shape the future before it shapes us. The future will grow out of the past by design or by accident. We can choose our preferred future based on the kingdom dream.

• Movement from participants to systems. Planning links the energies of individual members to the actions or goals of the entire congregation. Effective planning focuses scattered interests into a team ministry.

We support what we help create. Ideas developed by a few are usually implemented by only a few too. Plans made by a broad cross section of a congregation's members are more apt to become system-wide ministries. The old proverb, "The more, the merrier" applies well to planning.

• Movement from needs to resources. Planning mediates the movement from the push of human need to the pull of congregational resources. Needs and resources are matched up in planning. That's the genius of planning. In the words of actor Jack Albertson, "Success is the crossroads where opportunity and preparation meet."

In conclusion, planning is proactive and healthy. It's the polar opposite of problem solving, a reactive and unhealthy stance. When planning is described as movement, it reminds us the planner has the lever of initiative in his hands. The dreamer provides motivation and horsepower. But the planner selects directions and guides our futures.

Needs—What to Plan For

The needs to resources movement is an especially important planning dynamic. First, let's examine needs.

Needs assessment is basic to planning. Needs tell us what to plan for. Considerable information is available to help congregations profile the needs of their community. Census data, municipal planning agencies, and community development groups provide a mass of material on what a community is like and what it needs. For example, census data show the age groupings of a neighborhood and offer a clue to whether day-care or senior adult ministries is more appropriate as a church ministry.

One tool to assist a church in becoming more aware of the needs of its own members is the psychohistory profile. Such a profile isolates some typical life issues along age grouping lines. Clusters of age grouping generally signal a promising arena of ministry. Four selected issues illustrate the broad-based needs revealed by a congregational psychohistory profile.

PSYCHOHISTORY PROFILE

AGES

ISSUES	0—1	2—4	4—6	6—12
RELIGIOUS NEEDS	Healthy discoveries of love and reliability of persons and the universe. Trustworthiness of God.	Discovery of limits and a sense of self-worth. Good *vs.* evil a practical issue.	Developing a sense of self-control. Discovery of wrong and need for forgiveness.	Establishing sense of personal achievement. Discovery of service, altruism, and good works.
DEVELOPMENTAL NEEDS	Learning to trust or mistrust, to get and give, to attain satisfaction.	Learning to be autonomous, shameful, and doubting, to hold and let go, to control bodily functions.	Learning to show initiative, face guilt, to make, to deal with attachment to parent of opposite sex.	Learning to show industry and face inferiority, to complete, to do tasks.
FAMILY NEEDS	Dealing with mobility and the lack of extended family contacts. Coping with the threat of divorce and the one-parent family.			
VOCATIONAL NEEDS	Toys may reveal parental expectations.		"When I grow up . . ." statements.	Occupational games of pretending.

AGES

ISSUES	13—20	18—35	35—55	55—up
RELIGIOUS NEEDS	Developing a sense of belonging. Establishing a personal, independent faith.	Stabilizing deep relationships. Growing a faith sturdy enough for adulthood, family, and professional demands.	Discovering a sense of self-renewal. Creating a clear focus for living.	Finding a sense of satisfaction, meaning, and purpose. Trusting the future to God and younger generations.
DEVELOP-MENTAL NEEDS	Learning one's identity or identity diffusion, to be, to be an independent, faithful, sexual, career person.	Learning to achieve intimacy or isolation, to love, to make commitments to others without losing oneself.	Learning to generate or be self-absorbed, to create, to develop new challenges.	Learning to feel integrity or disgust and despair, to discover, to transfer hope to others, to face aging, fixed income, and death.
FAMILY NEEDS	Crucial importance of peer group.	Selecting a spouse or choosing singleness. Adjusting to marriage. Child bearing. Family is focus of some wives. Threat of divorce.	Child rearing. Child launching. Wife's career. Returning father. Switch-40s.	Empty nest. Retirement adjustments. Single partner after spouse's death.
VOCATION-AL NEEDS	Tentative choice of a lifework. Part-time jobs give taste of work world.	Vocational moratorium. Work is focus of husband and wife. Search for mentors. Commit to a career.	Becoming one's own person. Becoming a mentor. Risking new career ventures.	Moving from leadership to follower-ship. Retirement. Second career.

```
┌─────────────────────────────────────────────────────────┐
│                   ACTION EXERCISE #12                      │
│                                                            │
│            Discovering Congregational Age Needs            │
│                                                            │
│   1.  What percentage of our congregation fits into each age │
│       group?                                               │
│   2.  What are the three largest age groups?               │
│   3.  What are the special needs and concerns of these     │
│       largest age groups?                                  │
│   4.  What is our church providing currently to minister to │
│       these special needs? What else could be provided?    │
│   5.  What are the unique strengths of these largest age   │
│       groups that can be used as ministry resources?       │
└─────────────────────────────────────────────────────────┘
```

Strong ministry to strategic needs helps a congregation minister effectively and appropriately. A psychohistory profile of your church may help you focus on key ministry issues with more awareness and confidence. Healthy ministry is the product of planning to meet real needs.

Resources—What to Plan With

Resources are also basic to planning. Resources tell us what we have to plan with. Any church has a range of resources—members, property, offerings, information, and the like. But human resources are the most important resource of all. Without people, a congregation ceases to exist.

The health cycle model lends itself to evaluating human resources. Each stage of the cycle has church members who seem to relate to it most naturally. Assigning persons to the nine stages offers a subjective picture of a congregation's human resources. For example, church members who resonate with the dream stage are the congregation's visionaries. Name them. Visionaries are a valuable human resource—perhaps the most valuable group in any church.

Make nine lists of members' names. Head these lists with the general terms, "visionaries," "theologians," and the other terms on the chart. Assigning some persons to a single list may be difficult. But place each name on the list which seems to be the best overall designation of that person at the present.

Here's how to interpret your nine lists. The first six lists indicate persons who will minister with you. They are your congregation's most positive human resources. Even the traditionalists are valuable because they can signal when organizational slippage has begun.

Within the first six lists, note the longer lists. They represent your congregation's primary "people strengths" for ministry. The long lists name the folk who make your church productive. On the other hand, any short lists between "visionaries" to "traditionalists" indicate a training and development need. Short lists show you where to concentrate your training efforts.

ACTION EXERCISE #13

Human Resource Survey

1. Who are our congregation's visionaries?
    Theologians? Directors? Organizers?
    Activists? Traditionalists? Detectives?
    Fighters? Apathetic?
2. What are the largest groups? What do they signify?
    What do they provide our congregation?
3. What are the three smallest groups? What do they signify? What do they provide our congregation?
4. Overall, how would I describe the human resource and training picture in our church? What plans are appropriate now?

The final three lists—the detectives, the fighters, and the apathetic—identify members who need the ministry of their own

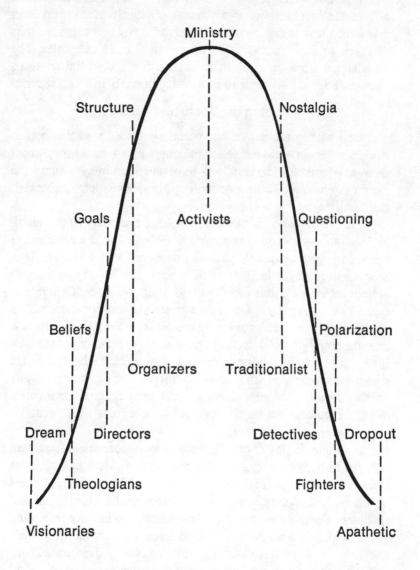

congregation. Whether these lists are long or short, their meaning is different. Long lists here aren't assets, obviously. Neither do short lists necessarily indicate trainable persons. Healthy congregations will tend to have shorter lists in these final three categories. The basic signal from the final three groups is simple: Minister to us first or we are unlikely ever to join you in ministry to others again.

Planning for Doors and Dreams

One participant group of special significance to planners is new members in a church. New members may assume they know their new church's dream; long-term members may assume the dream is obvious. Those two assumptions, when left unchecked, can begin an erosion of the dream.

Picture the problem like this. Visualize each stage of the health cycle as a door to your congregation. Potentially, a new member could enter your church through any of these doors. For example, a new member might identify with a goal, like increasing Sunday School attendance, and enter through that goal door. Or a ministry, like deaf ministry. Or even a nostalgic identification with a building or a minister, evoking memories from the past. So the new member joins your church through that door and may not see how his favorite goal or ministry or memory connects to the dream. He doesn't discover the uniqueness of his new congregation. Quite unintentionally, he helps dissipate the congregation's resources. Why? Because he has no concept of the core from which goals or ministries grow.

A solution to the doors issue is a new member orientation plan tailored to each congregation's special dream. Most new member orientation programs major on what time the Sunday School meets or where to find the choir rehearsal room or denominational distinctives. These items may be needed. But the healthy beginning point is the dream. New members need to discover how their church's dream came to life and how it has been lived out. Then, using the dream as a stackpole, the program elements of ministry, education, music, and the like can be fitted in.

Dominion Heights Church has designed a new member orientation program around their dream. Several times each year on three consecutive Sunday evenings two-hour sessions are staged. The first session centers on the kingdom dream of Dominion Heights Church. Testimonies of long-term members and slides guide new members through an overview of the unique development of this congregation.

The second session focuses on the inward journey of the dream. Worship, Bible study, and retreats are some of Dominion Heights' resources to stimulate spiritual growth.

The final session pivots around the outward journey of witness, mission, and community ministries. In fact, one mission support group guides Dominion Heights' new member orientation program. By helping new members discover their congregation's dream, this mission support group finds the doors to both the journey inward and journey outward easier to open for newcomers.

Planning: The Health Skill

TV newsman Dan Rather's wife describes him as a man who has visions but never plans. Dreams are the roots for plans. Plans are the fruit of dreams. Planning is the skill behind congregational health. Whether your church is an Old First, a growing suburban one, or a rural family chapel, the process is basic. Congregational health teams dreaming with planning.

Dreams without plans are fantasies. Plans without dreams are adrift. A dream and a plan are essential for congregational health. Plans translate our kingdom dream into concrete ministry. And, after all, that's the mission of Christ's church today.

Afterword

Thomas Jefferson once hoped aloud that America would have a revolution every twenty years. Jefferson wasn't advocating overthrow of the government. He envisioned no battles, no new flags, or any prisoners of war. Jefferson wanted a redefining of America for every new generation.

No church is healthy without a defined kingdom dream. Congregations either redefine their basic purpose every generation or they die. The road to health is to dream again.

Charles A. Lindbergh stated our hope:

> We actually live today
>   in our dreams of yesterday;
>   and, living in these dreams,
> we dream again.

The gospel of Christ's kingdom hasn't changed. We have only to dream it again.

APPENDIX A:
Systemic Theology: An Introduction to Some Assumptions for a New Theology

Systemic theology is a theology of the visible church and the corporate congregation as stated in 1 Corinthians 12's "body of Christ" metaphor. Systemic theology describes the synergistic, interactional, and interdependent expression of the church as organization. Both the institutional entity of the local congregation as well as the corporate team of believers are the concern of systemic theology.

Systemic theology and organizational behavior focus on "the church of the pastoral letters rather than the church of the Pauline Epistles. It is the church of extended duration rather than the church of the imminent return. It is the church with a ministry to its members and a mission to its age rather than a church which simply waits for its Lord to return. It is a church with polity, politics, prayer and program. It has a purpose for its being and a plan for its life." (H. Newton Malony, "Toward a Theology for Organization Development," *Christian Ministry,* July, 1975, p. 20.)

Systemic theology builds on this premise: Since God wants healthy congregations, then theology has organizational applications and organizations have theological foundations.

1. *Systemic Theology Assumption: The kingdom of God is a possible, redemptive dream.*

Organizational Dynamics Corollary: Healthy organizations

keep their purpose clearly defined and constantly visible to their participants.

Jesus inaugurated the kingdom of God (Mark 1:15). He spoke of this kingdom—of God ruling over persons and their institutions—more than any other issue. It was the subject of most of his parables. The kingdom of God was the dream of Jesus; it remains the redemptive vision of his followers.

The kingdom of God blends individual and corporate dimensions as well as local and universal expressions of redemptive ministry into a kingdom dream. The redemptive dream of God's kingdom on earth is both the goal and the product of believer's lives and congregation's mission.

2. *Systemic Theology Assumption: A kingdom dream binds persons together into a redeemed and a redeeming community.*

Organizational Dynamics Corollary: Healthy organizations are able to grow and change.

People with a vision of the kingdom of God have experienced grace and are concerned for the brokenness of others. A kingdom community is able to open itself to other persons and institutions and to accommodate itself to new challenges and opportunities (Acts 10—11).

3. *Systemic Theology Assumption: The ministry of redemption joins God and persons in co-mission.*

Organizational Dynamics Corollary: Healthy organizations utilize team effort.

God has called us to be his partners in creation (Gen. 1:26-30; 2:4-15) and re-creation (Matt. 28:19-20). We are on commission with God in the work of redemption. We witness to God's salvation; God saves persons. People are the primary resource of any church and must be valued as God's crowning creation and the object of his redemption.

4. *Systemic Theology Assumption: Spiritual gifts have a corporate application.*

Organizational Dynamics Corollary: Healthy organizations are creative stewards of all their human and physical resources.

Paul's "body of Christ" metaphor reminds us of the diverse gifts available within the corporate congregation (1 Cor. 12—13; Rom. 12:4-8; Eph. 4:11-14). Unity for a church is in its kingdom dream. Using all resources on kingdom priorities by plan is the ever-present management challenge for church leaders. No Christian is complete in isolation. The community of supportive believers and the challenge of the world are necessary for maximum growth and mature ministry.

5. *Systemic Theology Assumption: The range of human experience can be understood by the theological categories of life, death, and resurrection.*

Organizational Dynamics Corollary: Healthy organizations are dynamic, changing, and oriented toward growth.

Persons and organizations go through a cycle of birth, growth, maturity, decline, and, (if they do not take action toward renewal) death. The possibility of rebirth is always present, since organizational death and spiritual death are not the same phenomena.

6. *Systemic Theology Assumption: Sin corrupts and taints even divine-human institutions like the church.*

Organizational Dynamics Corollary: Healthy organizations constantly dream, evaluate, and plan.

The fact of sin tempers institutional optimism. It's realistic to recogize that organizational renewal will forever remain a need within congregations. A church perpetually requires internal feedback and the ministry of variance sensors in order to stay healthy.

7. *Systemic Theology Assumption: Church revitalization concentrates on the life of the visible, institutional congregation as well as the invisible, mystical church.*

Organizational Dynamics Corollary: Healthy organizations develop strategies for institutional renewal.

Congregations are both living organizations and supernatural organisms. A healthy church maintains its institutional vitality by a variety of deliberate revival and renewal efforts. These renewal efforts try to create a climate in which the Holy Spirit can be active.

Appendix B:
Glossary of Terms

Controlling images: the core of personal faith

Credo: Latin for "I believe." When used in reference to preaching, it denotes a vehicle for publicly stating one's redemptive dream.

Dream: the underlying vision that gives an organization or institution its unique purpose and personality

Ecclesiola in ecclesia: Luther's phrase describing a "church within a church" like the informal organization that exists in most congregations without matching the formal organizational chart

Energy reservoir: a person or group's enthusiasm and vigor for projects or programs; a major clue to personal motivation and organizational climate

Experiential belief system: the unconsciously lived aspects of personal faith that are usually spontaneous, intuitive, repetitious, and corporate

Grapevine: the informal communication system in an organization

Informal organization: emerges spontaneously to meet relational needs; opposite of formal organization which is designed primarily to accomplish tasks as goals

Interface: the boundaries where separate organizational entities meet

Intervention: an action taken after organizational diagnosis to turn the institution toward its missional purpose

Kingdom stories: the parables of Jesus as they reveal his redemptive dream for persons and their institutions

Norm: the unspoken and unwritten patterns, habits, and traditions of an organization; unconscious practices that give an organization many of its unique features

Nostalgia: a sense of homesickness which when expressed in an organizational context is an early warning sign of loss of the dream

Organization development: planned organizational change, usually from the top down

Organizational drift: when an organization's mission is never defined, becomes dulled, or is lost and it operates without clear reference to its dream

Organizational "rent": the congregation's (sometimes costly) expectations and demands on their minister to provide and maintain basic ministry roles and functions

Provolutionary model: a picture of an organization's life cycle in stages with special attention given to "turning toward the future" via planned revitalization

Psychohistory profile: cross-referencing and analyzing a congregation's needs over and against developmental tasks

Regenerative system: an organization with high degrees of trust, openness, and stakeholding and with low risk in experimenting; opposite of a degenerative system

Stakeholder: any member of a volunteer organization who has an emotional stake in the organization's health and direction; parallels the stockholder in publicly owned corporations

Systemic theology: a theology of the visible church as stated in 1 Corinthians 12 "body of Christ" metaphor and in other relevant biblical, historical, and contemporary materials; depicts the local congregation as a social system

Task force: a temporary organizational unit which is designed to complete a project or solve a problem; usually an ad hoc or throwaway organization

Variance sensors: persons who usually function on the fringes of institutional life but because of their basic loyalty to the organization are often sensitive to its relationship to its basic dream

Volunteer organization: any organization whose participants choose freely and intentionally to join and serve